Bike VICTORIA

**Your guide to 55 rides in
and around Victoria and beyond**

Revised edition

John Crouch

Chickadee Press
Victoria, BC

Disclaimer
The author and publisher have made every attempt to be as accurate as possible in describing the rides within this book. However, they relinquish all responsibility for changes that may have occurred to roadways and trails since the book's date of publication.

Library and Archives Canada Cataloguing in Publication
Crouch, John, 1941–
    Bike Victoria :Your guide to 55 rides in and around Victoria and beyond, revised edition / John Crouch.
Includes index.
ISBN 978-0-9731913-4-9
    1. Bicycle touring—British Columbia—Victoria Region—Guidebooks.
2. Victoria Region (B.C.)—Guidebooks. I. Title.

GV1046.C32V53 2006   796.6'4'0971128   C2006-901486-8

Cover and book design: Frances Hunter, Beacon Hill Communications Group
Front cover photograph: Brenda Nelson
Back cover photograph: John Luton
Frontispiece: Lochside Drive/Trail, Sidney
Maps: Amy Rutherford
Photographs: Mia Crouch, Jeff George, John Luton, James Smith and Dan van Stolk. All other photographs are by the author

Cover photograph: Esquimalt Lagoon

First printing, May, 2012
Second printing, January, 2014

Chickadee Press
303–1137 View Street
Victoria, BC Canada
V8V 3L9

For Lorinda

Acknowledgements

I've been fortunate over the years to work with a core group of people in the creation of my guidebooks. This revised edition is no exception.

Frances Hunter, as always, has designed a clear, simple yet aesthetically satisfying book. Amy Rutherford's maps are unfussy and easy to follow. Brian Connon's editing is thorough and indispensable. Mia Crouch, my daughter, provided photos that are perfect for the book's purpose. I appreciate them all and thank them.

I'd like to thank Kim Gard who, on our Friday morning rides, accompanied me on all the new routes. Rain or shine, her cheerfulness and enthusiasm were a bonus to my rides. I also thank Chris Paul, an arborist and cyclist, who gave his time and expertise to one of the book's new rides, and John Luton, Victoria's foremost cycling advocate, who provided photos and encouragement.

To all my friends and "passers-by" who were willing subjects for the photos, I thank them all.

Contents

The Rides (from point of origin)

Victoria, Oak Bay and Esquimalt

Saanich, Central Saanich, North Saanich & Sidney

West Shore (View Royal, Colwood, Langford, Highlands, Metchosin and Sooke)

Roads and Trails (All rides start and finish west of the Johnson Street Bridge)

Beyond (Shawnigan Lake, Mill Bay, Cowichan Bay and the Cowichan Valley)

Trails

Routes to Victoria from:

Index

Preface to the Revised Edition

In this revised and expanded edition of *Bike Victoria* I've added eight new rides intended to broaden the scope of routes available to riders who live in or visit Victoria and its surrounding communities. The routes I'm most pleased to include are those under the title Roads and Trails. These are for riders who like loop routes, over a mix of surfaces and terrain, and prefer, or have, a bike other than a road bike. Two short, urban rides, the Arborist's Ride and the Coffee Shop Crawl, I hope will become favourites. A shorter Wine Tour that visits seven wineries is included plus the trail over the now open Kinsol Trestle.

Introduction

I've owned a bike since I was a child. I recall my father rather ingeniously converting a woman's bike into a contraption his eight-year old son could ride. I had lots of fun with that bike but it wasn't until my early teens did I get a "real bike." My first traffic violation was on that bike. It was a cold winter's evening and I was riding with some friends for something to do. My front, battery operated, light had just given out when a policeman, on his bike, (this was in England) stopped me and told me that since I had no functioning front light, I had to walk — which I did — until he rode out of sight. I then got on my bike and began riding home. The "bobby," being rather crafty and knowing the indolence of young teenage boys, decided to back-track to check on my progress. All of a sudden, he was by my side ordering me to stop and get off my bike. He promptly cuffed me on the side of my head and said if I didn't obey the law he'd report me to my parents. Needless to say, I complied.

It took almost half a century from riding my first makeshift bike to tour and explore the seemingly endless number of roads in and around Victoria and those of southern Vancouver Island. I've ridden some of the routes many times and never get tired of experiencing the pleasure of such outings no matter what the season.

And the seasons bring their own distinctive ingredients to the rides. The sun rising over the Cascade Mountains on a winter's early morning ride is a wondrous sight — the burnt-red sun glowing with the mountains silhouetted black on the horizon.

In spring, the subtle aromas of blooming plants, shrubs and trees dissipate any lingering winter blues and by summer, the avenues of fresh-leafed trees, hedgerows and lush gardens and fields make us want to ride longer and make picnics a delightful punctuation of the day's outing.

Though not as vivid as the colours of the fall in colder climes, the autumnal shades we experience here are, nevertheless, lovely. There's nothing quite like the pinkish blush of the dogwood leaves or the broad-leafed maple and chestnut leaves turning yellow and orange to evoke the bitter-sweet feeling that winter is almost upon us bringing its dramatic sunrises.

Included in this revised edition is an expanded selection of rides that will last anywhere from half an hour to two or three hours. There are, of course, longer rides and at least three that are suggested for the hard-core road-bike specialist. My intention has been to have rides that will suit all levels of riding ability and moods. There is no area of Victoria and the surrounding municipalities and districts that doesn't have at least one ride passing through it.

One last word. Terrain. Situated as it is by the ocean and encompassed by hills, the Victoria area is not flat. Almost everywhere you go, be it in the city, the suburbs or the surrounding countryside, you're confronted with hills. It's a given and you have to accept it. There are, mercifully, exceptions — and they are significant. Due to the ingenuity of railway engineers who restricted local railway grades to no more than 2%, the railway corridors that once were in profusion in and around Victoria, now provide the flattest rides in the book.

I hope that the wide selection of routes offered in this revised book will both entice all those who love getting out on their bikes to explore these options, and encourage others who don't ride to "have a go."

How to use this book

All the ride descriptions follow a similar pattern — with a few exceptions. Each ride is given an introduction and is intended to give a brief summation of what you're likely to see and/or experience on the ride. Sometimes I'll give some history of the area or a biographical note or simply write about the terrain. The introduction is intended to whet your appetite for the ride.

General description I've tried to describe succinctly the ride in a sentence or two, giving a hint of what's in store.

Location This refers to the ride's geographic location within the context of greater Victoria.

Length Because the metric system is the official measurement of distance in Canada, all the rides are measured in kilometres. For riders not used to this system, just remember that a kilometre is .6 of a mile (or vice verse, a mile is 1.6 kilometres). The majority of the rides in the book are loop courses with the rest being out-and-back. (I've assumed that riders will have a computer on their bikes although having one is not necessary.)

Level This is probably the most important piece of information for the majority of riders. Although I don't go into detail, the three designations: easy; moderate and strenuous will, I hope, enable you to choose a ride that suits your fitness level. Remember, apart from a few exceptions, there are always some ups and downs in most of the rides. Even though a ride might be described as easy, it will invariably have some change in elevation along its route. The major exceptions are the two regional trails.

Start This is the exact location where you'll start, and, in most cases, finish, the ride. Where possible I've started rides in places with lots of parking.

Highlights Here, I've indicated what I think might appeal to riders in the way of sites, terrain and places to stop and eat or picnic.

How to get there I've made the assumption that, apart from those rides starting in downtown Victoria, riders will take their bikes to the start by car. (This is not to preclude the idea of riding to a ride's start.) The directions are given from Victoria's centre. A map of the city and area would be a useful addition to my directions.

The ride You'll notice the format is simple. There is the checkpoint, e.g. (5), with the number of kilometres, in brackets, e.g. (7.3 km),* covered from the ride's beginning. Then follows written directions that correspond to the accompanying map's checkpoint. Always compare what you read with what you're seeing on the map. The language of the directions is to the point — right becomes **R** and left, **L**.

* These numbers may vary according to tire pressure, computer quality and computer calibration on different bikes.

Safe Cycling

The first principle of cycling on roads, in my mind, is to behave as if you belong there. And you do. But what does that mean? Well, you ride according to the rules of the road (see below); you ride confidently; you ride with knowledge of good bike handling; you make eye contact with vehicle drivers, other cyclists and pedestrians at intersections and driveways; you ride defensively; you ride with awareness of what is going on around you and you ride conspicuously, i.e. wearing bright colours and reflective clothing.

According to the province's *Motor Vehicle Act* (RSBC 1996, Chapter 318 — part 3), a cyclist has the same rights and duties as a driver of a motor vehicle. Here are some other requirements of the act as it pertains to cyclists.

A cyclist:

- must not ride on a sidewalk unless directed to by official signage;
- must ride as near as practicable to the right side of the road except when turning left or overtaking;
- must not ride two abreast on the roadway;
- is not required to ride on any part of a road that is not paved;
- must use lights — white in front, red at the back — during hours of darkness;
- must have good brakes;
- must wear a safety approved helmet securely fastened and properly fitted.

Readers wishing to read a more precise and complete version of the act can do so at their local library or obtain a copy of the Greater Victoria Cycling Coalition's booklet *Bike Sense* (their website is: **http://bikesense.bc.ca**) and read the chapter, Cyclist and the Law.

Area map showing rides by number

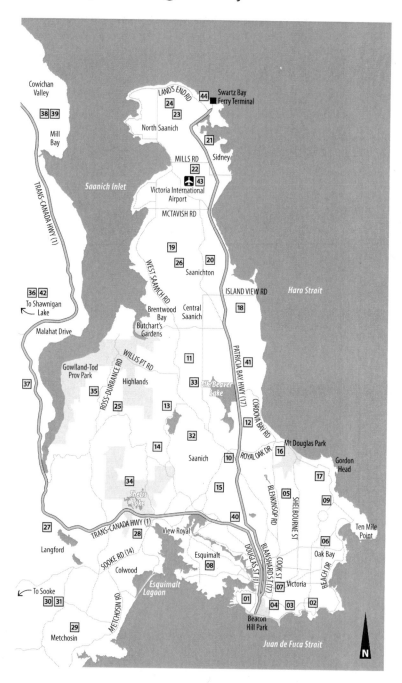

Adapting this book to be more user-friendly

You've noticed, I'm sure, that when a paperback gets a lot of use the spine slowly disintegrates and pages start to fall out. This is especially true of guidebooks when they are constantly being referred to.

A trick I learned many years ago was that as soon as I bought a guidebook, I'd take it to my favourite photocopying store and have them spiral bind the thing. It works like a charm. You open the guide at the selected page and fold it over. The pages are individually kept in place by the plastic spiral not the glue. This way the book will last forever — almost.

Map legend

— Route

– – Alternate route

Route direction arrows

Roads

Highways

Trail or path

Railway

Streams and rivers

Bodies of water

Parks

Private parks and golf courses

North marker

S | **F** Start/Finish of route

S Start of route (if different from finish)

F Finish of route (if different from start)

① Checkpoints

5 Distance in kilometres

Ⓐ Suggested rides

■ Point of interest or landmark

B Beach access

Airport

T Toilets

P Parking

Café or Pub

Marina

Vineyard

14 Tree of interest

Victoria, Oak Bay and Esquimalt

1

DOWNTOWN VICTORIA / JAMES BAY

As the shortest ride in the book, it acts rather like a touristic ride through some of the oldest historical areas of Victoria and some of its most picturesque.

Almost immediately you pass modern tall hotel and apartment buildings but if you look to your right before crossing Blanshard Street you'll notice the century-old wooden structure of the Church of Our Lord. It was built as a reaction to the "ritualizing" of the Anglican church by a Reverend Cridge in 1872. He called it a Reformed Episcopal church. Across the road, and you'll ride right past it, is the splendid buildings and gardens of St. Ann's Academy. Now owned and preserved by the provincial government, its origins go back to the late 1800s and it was the sisters of St. Ann and the Roman Catholic priest, the Reverend Modeste Demers who started work on the present buildings in 1871.

Beacon Hill Park is the city's oldest park having been estab-lished, in a formal way, in 1882. Beforehand it had been part of the Hudson's Bay Company land and had become known as Beacon Hill because of the two navigational beacons situated there. Today it's a mixture of for-mal and open parkland and gives the city a panoramic opening to the ocean and the mountains beyond.

As you ride west along Dallas Road you enter James Bay. Victoria's most famous artist, Emily Carr, lived in the neighbourhood — her home being on Simcoe Street and the family home on Government Street. In the mid-1800s James Bay blossomed into Victoria's most fashionable suburb where the rich and influential built large houses on large parcels of land. It's no longer the sole domain of the rich and famous but as a collection of old and new developments it has an appeal that many visitors appreciate.

General description

A short loop ride that passes some of Victoria's most famous landmarks.

Location Downtown Victoria, Beacon Hill Park and James Bay.

Length 7 kilometres.

Level Easy.

Start Downtown: The corner of Humboldt Street and Douglas Street.

Highlights Historical buildings; Mile "0" and the Terry Fox statue in Beacon Hill Park; Ogden Point Café; Fisherman's Wharf.

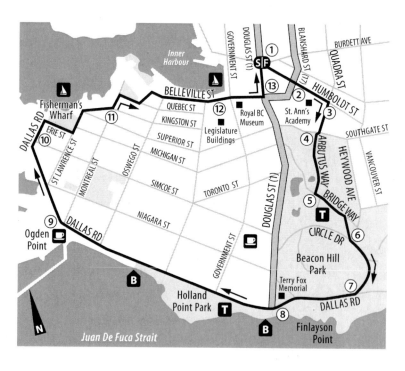

THE RIDE

①   From the corner of Humboldt and Douglas Streets ride east on Humboldt passing tall hotel and apartment buildings.

②   (0.2 km)   At the traffic light cross Blanshard Street. The historical St. Ann's Academy and its Heritage Garden are accessed about 200 metres along Humboldt on your **R**.

③   (0.5 km)   Turn **R** onto Quadra Street.

④   (0.7 km)   Cross Southgate Street and enter Beacon Hill Park up the Arbutus Way entrance. At the top bear **L** onto Bridge Way.

⑤   (1.01 km)   After 100 metres turn **R** on Bridge Way as it continues to Circle Drive.

⑥   (1.04 km)   Turn **L** onto Circle Drive.

⑦   (1.09 km)   Turn **R** onto Dallas Road.

⑧   (2.04 km)   Bear **L** as Dallas and Douglas meet. Mile "0" is at this intersection as is the Terry Fox memorial statue.

⑨   (3.08 km)   Pass Ogden Point Café and the Port of Victoria on your **L**.

⑩   (4.07 km)   Bear **R** onto Erie Street and then after 100 metres bear **L** onto St. Lawrence Street. Fisherman's Wharf is on your **L**.

⑪   (5.0 km)   Cross Superior Street at the stop sign to take Kingston Street on your **R**. After 200 metres bear **L** onto Montreal Street then **R** onto Quebec Street and **L** again onto Pendray which becomes Belleville Street.

⑫   (6.0 km)   You'll pass in front of the BC Legislature Building on your **R**.

⑬   (6.02 km)   Turn **L** at the second traffic light on to Douglas Street back to your ride's start.

DOWNTOWN VICTORIA / FAIRFIELD / HARLING POINT

Like the previous ride, this route starts in downtown Victoria but heads east rather than west as the first ride does. You soon encounter Cook Street Village — a neighbourhood gathering place replete with pub, cafés, bakery, grocery and other stores — all you'd need to feel part of a community.

Once on the waterfront you get the expansive views of the Strait of Juan de Fuca and the Olympic Mountains beyond. And, you'll ride past Victoria's most significant cemetery: the Ross Bay Cemetery. Charles Ross was Fort Victoria's first agent and it was his widow, Isabel Ross, along with her second husband, Joseph Despard Pemberton, who owned the land and named the bay. The government, needing more cemetery space (Pioneer Square on Quadra Street being "full" by the early 1870s), bought five hectares of the waterfront property and created what it hoped would be a very picturesque, "English-style" cemetery. If James Bay was the home to Victoria's late 1800s, early 1900s rich and famous, Ross Bay Cemetery became their graveyard.

Hollywood Crescent takes its name from Thomas Shotbolt and his wife's 4-hectare estate and mansion on Gonzales Hill. Shotbolt was one of three pioneer pharmacists in Victoria. His success as a businessman was reflected in the Victorian splendor of the family's home which was named Hollywood.

As you head toward Harling Point at the bottom of Crescent Road you encounter the spacious Chinese Cemetery. Chosen for its harmonious fusion of natural elements in 1903, the Chinese community wanted the land as a temporary resting place for their dead. Custom was that eventually the remains would be taken back to China for final burial. Shortly before the Second World War it was no longer possible to transport remains back to China and so, in 1961, Chinese bones from across Canada were brought to Victoria and are interred here.

General description

A loop route that goes from downtown, through Cook Street Village, to the waterfront. You'll pass two historically significant cemeteries; ride through the pleasant streets of the Fairfield neighbourhood and skirt Beacon Hill Park on your way back.

Location   Downtown, Fairfield's waterfront, Harling Point.

Length   11 kilometres.

Level   Easy.

Start   The corner of Humboldt and Douglas Street in downtown Victoria.

Highlights   Cook Street Village; the waterfront; the Ross Bay and Chinese cemeteries; Harling Point's rocks.

Dallas Road with Trial Island in the distance.

THE RIDE

①   From the corner of Humboldt and Douglas Streets ride east on Humboldt to cross Blanshard Street 200 metres away.

②   (0.2 km)   Between Blanshard and Quadra Streets is the access to the historical St. Ann's Academy and its Heritage Gardens.

③   (0.5 km)   Cross the traffic-lighted Quadra Street.

④   (0.7 km)   Turn **R** off Humboldt onto Vancouver Street then, after 100 metres turn **L** at the four-way stop onto Southgate Street.

⑤   (1.01 km)   Turn **R** onto Cook Street. The village starts here for three blocks.

⑥   (2.0 km)   Turn **L** onto Dallas Road — Beacon Hill Park is on your **R**. You'll now ride along the waterfront for a few kilometres.

⑦   (3.0 km)   The historically significant Ross Bay Cemetery is now on your **L**. After about a kilometre Dallas Road becomes Hollywood Crescent.

⑧   (4.07 km)   Turn **R** onto Ross Street. Gonzales Bay is on your **R** at which point Ross Street becomes Crescent Road.

⑨   (5.04 km)   Turn **R** to continue on Crescent Road (to bear **L** at this point would take you up the steep King George Terrace). At the bottom of Crescent turn **L** onto Penzance Road. The Chinese Cemetery is on the **R** along Penzance.

⑩   (5.09 km)   Although Penzance has no exit there is a trail that joins Maquinna Road — take it. Ride the short Maquinna and take Lorne Terrace, the last street on the **L**.

⑪   (6.05 km)   After a short jog **R** off Lorne, turn **L** onto Crescent. You are now on your way back to town.

⑫   (7.05 km)   Having ridden back along Crescent and continued on along Ross Street turn **R** onto St. Charles.

⑬   (7.07 km)   Turn **L** onto Fairfield Road. Fairfield Plaza is a few metres on your **R** along Fairfield. Ross Bay Cemetery is on your **L**. (Ross Bay Villa is also on your **R** opposite the cemetery and is dedicated as an information/archive centre for the cemetery).

⑭	(8.02 km)	Turn **L** onto Memorial Crescent immediately after the cemetery. After about 100 metres turn **R** onto May Street.
⑮	(9.04 km)	Follow May Street to its end and turn **R** onto Cook Street and then turn onto Park Boulevard 50 metres on the **L**.
⑯	(9.07 km)	At the top of Park turn **R** onto Heyward Avenue. Beacon Hill Park is on your **L**.
⑰	(10.01 km)	Turn **L** onto Southgate Street.
⑱	(10.06 km)	At the first traffic-light turn **R** onto Douglas Street taking care to follow the Highway #1 sign (Douglas Street) and not the Highway #17 sign (Blanshard Street). You now ride down the hill to your start at Humboldt.

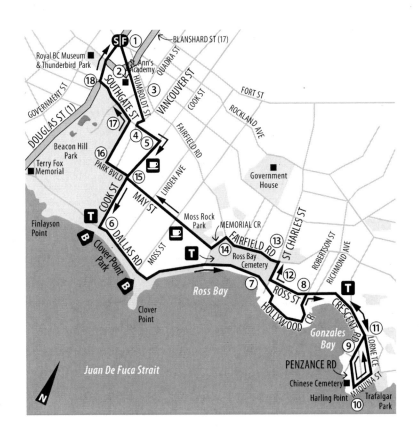

3

COFFEE SHOP CRAWL

Neighbourhoods are what make cities livable. They're smaller, more intimate and manageable parts of the whole often with their own singular attractiveness. San Francisco and Portland to our south are classic examples of neighbourhood cities. In fact, Victoria is sometimes referred to as "Little Portland." During this short ride (it's just shy of 20 kilometres) you'll pass through all the established neighbourhoods that create what we call Victoria — Fairfield, Fernwood, James Bay, Vic West and Oak Bay. (Although Oak Bay is a municipality in its own right, many regard it as a natural extension of the city.) As you can see from the route's description, I've chosen to point out most of the coffee shops/cafes/ bakeries along the way (thus the ride's title.) You can stop at all, some, one or none at all. For those who don't drink coffee, think of the

ride as a neighbourhood tour (or "noodle" as I like to call my leisurely-paced rides).

I envision the route to be a way for riders to get to know parts of the city they might not otherwise visit. Although I've put the start and finish of the ride on the edge of downtown, you can begin (and finish) at any point of the route, especially if you live in one of the neighbourhoods.

(Note: I've attempted to be current with business names, however, they can change over time or even cease to exist.)

General description   A circle ride that passes through all the city's established neighbour- hoods. Most, if not all of the coffee shops "enroute" are noted plus three bakeries.

Location   Victoria's four main neighbourhoods: Fairfield, Fernwood, James Bay and Vic. West plus Oak Bay.

Off again — after coffee.

Length 20 kilometres

Level Easy

Start Fishermen's Wharf off St. Lawrence Street

Highlights All the coffee you can drink. All the baked goodies you can consume (on your own dime, that is). Some of the best urban landscape in North America.

THE RIDE

① With Fishermen's Wharf behind you, ride up Dallas Road on the **L** of the Shoal Point condominium building and turn **R** onto the continuation of Dallas.

② (1.5 km) Turn **L** onto Boyd Street and then **R** onto Niagara Street.

③ (1.9 km) Turn **L** onto Menzies Street. You're now entering the heart of James Bay. The James Bay Coffee Company and Discovery Coffee are located here.

④ (2.1 km) At the four-way stop turn **R** onto the one-way Simcoe Street. (The last house on the **L** before Douglas Street is Emily Carr's "House of All Sorts" which she built in 1913.)

⑤ (2.7 km) Cross Douglas Street and bear **L** to enter Beacon Hill Park on Circle Drive. (The Beacon Drive In is one block to your **R** on Douglas.)

⑥ (3.2 km) Pass the Children's Farm on your **R** and then turn **L** onto Heywood Way. After the cricket pitch turn **R** onto Park Boulevard.

⑦ (3.7 km) Turn **L** onto Cook Street. In less than 100 metres you're in Cook Street Village. On your **L** are Serious Coffee and Starbucks. On your **R** are the Moka House and Bubby's Kitchen.

⑧ (4.0 km) Turn **R** onto Oscar Street.

⑨ (4.6 km) As Oscar dead ends at Moss Street take the path to Fairfield Road and turn **R**. (From May to October, the Moss Street Market installs itself across the road in Sir James Douglas School yard.) Continue on Fairfield going east.

⑩ (5.5 km) Pass Fairfield Plaza on your **L** and Ross Bay Cemetery on your **R**. You now ride up to and cross Foul Bay Road where Fairfield Road becomes Beach Drive.

⑪ (6.9 km) Turn **L** onto Mountjoy Avenue. You're now in Oak Bay.

⑫ (7.1 km) Turn **R** onto Central Avenue.

⑬ (7.4 km) At the stop sign turn **L** onto Victoria Avenue.

⑭ (7.8 km) Turn **R** onto McNeill Avenue. Across the street, at the corner of Roslyn Road, is the Demi-tasse Café.

⑮ (8.1 km) Turn **L** onto Monterey Avenue.

⑯ (8.8 km) At the traffic light turn **L** onto Oak Bay Avenue. This is Oak Bay Village. On the corner of Monterey and Oak Bay Avenue is Ottavio's. On your **R** as you head west are the Oak Bay Bistro and Starbucks.

⑰ (9.2 km) Turn **R** at the next light onto Elgin Road. As the road turns **R** to enter the public works yard you take the paved path on the **L** that leads to Goldsmith Street. Turn **L** onto Goldsmith and then **R** onto Bee Street riding past the Oak Bay Recreation Centre.

⑱ (10.1 km) Cross Cadboro Bay Road at the light onto Florence Street.

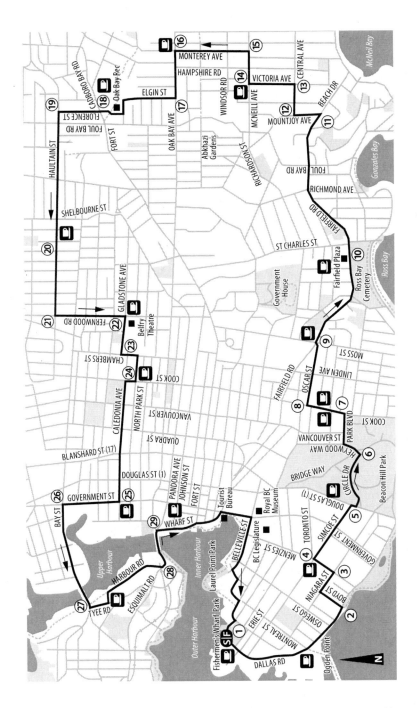

⑲	(10.4 km)	Turn **L** onto Haultain Street. Stay on Haultain crossing, on bike lanes, Richmond Road and Shelbourne Street.
⑳	(11.8 km)	Pass through Haultain Corners with the Koffi café on the **L**.
㉑	(12.1 km)	Turn **L** onto Fernwood Road at four-way stop.
㉒	(12.8 km)	Turn **R** onto the plaza in front of the Belfry Theatre. This is the centre of Fernwood. You'll find a collection of stores, a coffee shop, a pub, an art gallery and a restaurant. (Another restaurant is opposite the pub on Gladstone Avenue.)
㉓	(13.1 km)	Continue through the plaza on Gladstone and turn **L** onto Chambers Street. After two blocks turn **R** onto North Park Street opposite the community garden. The Parsonage Café is on your **L** just before Cook Street.
㉔	(13.5 km)	Turn **R** onto Cook and get ready to turn **L** onto Caledonia Avenue at the light. Keep on Caledonia past the police station and the Memorial Centre and, as the street becomes Chatham Street, cross Blanchard and Douglas streets.
㉕	(14.7 km)	Turn **R** onto Government Street. (Cascadia Bakery is close to this corner to your **L**.)
㉖	(15.1 km)	At the next light, turn **L** onto Bay Street.
㉗	(16.3 km)	After crossing the Bay Street Bridge turn **L** onto Tyee Road and **L** again onto Harbour Road. As you round the bend, on your **R** is the fol epi bakery and Caffé Fantastico. Continue on Harbour to its junction with Esquimalt Road.
㉘	(17.1 km)	Turn **L** onto Esquimalt Road and cross the Johnson Street Bridge. Over the bridge turn **R** onto Wharf Street. Pass Bastion Square on your **L**. You'll find a number of cafes and restaurants here and along Wharf.
㉙	(17.6 km)	At the Tourist Bureau turn **R** onto Government Street. At its junction with Belleville turn **R** and follow the twisting road back to St. Lawrence and the entrance to Fishermen's Wharf. The Moka House coffee shop is on the ground level of Shoal Point.

JAMES BAY / OAK BAY

This ride introduces you to what has become quintessential Victoria — historical buildings, large Victorian houses, immaculate homes and gardens, and a sweeping shoreline.

You'll pass the legislative building, the Inner Harbour, tour James Bay — one of Victoria's oldest neighbourhoods and ride through the popular Beacon Hill Park. There are two historically interesting cemeteries en route — Ross Bay Cemetery where many of the city's founders are buried, and Harling Point's Chinese Cemetery which was intended as a temporary burial site for the deceased before being returned to homeland China.

About halfway through the ride you'll enter Oak Bay via its beautifully-situated golf course and its marina. On the way back you pass the stately Government House (and yes, you can visit) and Cook Street's village where you'll find a good selection of coffee shops and a wonderful bakery.

General description A ride that combines buildings and places of historical interest with a route that takes you along part of the area's most pleasant shorelines.

Location Victoria's Beacon Hill Park, James Bay, Oak Bay, Rockland Avenue and Cook Street Village.

Length 21 kilometres.

Level Easy.

Start Beacon Hill Park's Children's Farm carpark.

Highlights Historical buildings and sites; ocean and mountain views; beautiful homes and gardens; good selection of cafés; Mile 0 with the memorial statue of Terry Fox.

How to get there From downtown take Douglas Street going south toward the ocean. Beacon Hill Park will be on your **L** after the Southgate Street intersection. Take the first **L** onto Circle Drive. The farm's carpark is about 200 metres on the **R**.

THE RIDE

①   Leave the Beacon Hill Park carpark adjacent to the Children's Farm turning **L** onto Circle Drive. After 200 metres turn **L** onto Douglas Street (Beacon Drive-In is across the road) and then **R** a few metres along Douglas onto Niagara Street.

② (0.7 km)   Turn **R** onto Government Street. Pass the James Bay Inn on your **L** at Toronto Street and then, at 1.5 km pass the legislative building on your **L** and the Royal BC Museum on the **R**.

③ (1.8 km)   Turn **L** onto Belleville Street to ride alongside the wall of the Inner Harbour. Follow this roadway as it curves along the coastline of James Bay's waterfront.

④ (2.8 km)   On the **R**, just past the stop sign at Superior Street, is Fisherman's Wharf. Continue to follow the curving road past the Canadian Coast Guard Station also on your **R**.

⑤ (3.9 km)   You're now on Dallas Road. Ogden Point and its eponymous café are on your **R**. Half a kilometre further on is Holland Point — a grassy headland that signals the beginning of Beacon Hill Park.

⑥ (5.4 km)   Here you'll pass, on the **L**, the mile "0" sign marking the beginning (or end) of the Trans-Canada Highway.

⑦ (7.5 km)   Ross Bay Cemetery is on your **L**.

⑧ (8.9 km)   Turn **R** onto Ross Street which quickly becomes Crescent Road.

⑨ (9.6 km)   Turn **R** down Crescent Road toward the ocean. This leads you to Harling Point and the Chinese Cemetery. You'll turn **L** at the cemetery along Penzance Road, at the end of which you'll turn **L** on a short narrow path to Maquinna Street. Continue on Maquinna and turn **L** at its end onto Lorne Terrace. Turn next **R** riding up the steep incline of King George Terrace.

⑩ (11.1 km)   Trafalgar Park is a viewpoint over the Strait of Juan de Fuca to the Olympic Mountains, Trial Island is below to the **L**.

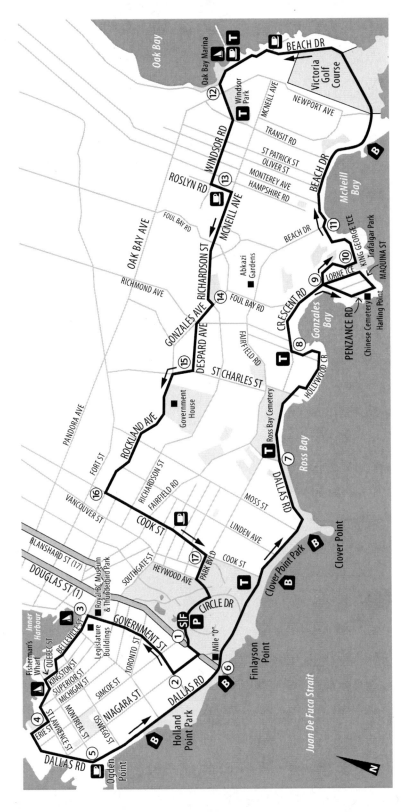

⑪	(11.6 km)	Turn **R** at the stop sign onto Beach Drive. At about 13 km the road bisects the beautifully situated Victoria Golf Course and at the 14 km is the Oak Bay Beach Hotel **R** with its English-style pub, the Snug. The Oak Bay Marina soon follows. Here you'll find a restaurant and café.
⑫	(14.8 km)	Turn **L** onto Windsor Road, Windsor Park is on your left.
⑬	(15.8 km)	Turn **L** onto Roslyn Road and then **R** onto McNeill Avenue. The Demitasse Café is at this corner. At a four-way crossing, McNeill becomes Richardson Road.
⑭	(17.0 km)	Turn **R** onto Gonzales Avenue and then, 200 metres further, cross Richmond Avenue to take Despard Avenue on your **L**.
⑮	(17.7 km)	Turn **R** onto St. Charles Street for 150 metres before turning **L** onto Rockland Avenue. You'll pass Government House shortly on your **L**.
⑯	(19.1 km)	Turn **L** at the traffic lights onto Cook Street. At the bottom of a slight hill you'll pass through Cook Street Village. This charming few blocks has a good selection of cafés and stores not to mention that wonderful bakery — Bubby Rose's.
⑰	(20.1 km)	Just past the village turn **R** onto Park Boulevard. Turn **L** at the stop sign onto Heywood Avenue and enter Beacon Hill Park. After 500 metres turn **R** onto Circle Drive riding the short distance back to the Children's Farm carpark.

BEACON HILL PARK / MOUNT DOUGLAS PARK / BROADMEAD

At slightly over 30 kilometres this ride covers an intriguing variety of neighbourhoods and parkland. After starting in Victoria's oldest and most loved park — Beacon Hill Park (so named for the two beacons erected on the hill in 1846 as nautical navigational guides), you head north through Cook Street village to ride eventually through the western edge of the Gordon Head neighbourhood.

Mount Douglas Park (Mt. Doug) is the next landmark of note. Although you won't ride into the heart of the park (its entrance road being a brutally steep 1.5 kilometre climb to the park's 227-metre summit) you'll ride along its beautifully wooded eastern boundary. The park is named after Sir James Douglas, British Columbia's first governor-general, who in 1858 established the land as a park. The park's

mount is known geologically as a monadnock — tough, rock material that withstood the powerful etching forces of the last ice-age. (Other monadnocks in the area include Mt. Finlayson, Mt. Newton, Mt. Tolmie and Bear Hill.)

Following Mt. Doug you'll ride through the attractive suburb of Broadmead. Over the thirty-odd years since its completion, the residents of this community have assiduously concentrated on keeping the forest and green spaces that were originally envisioned for this suburb. You'll ride past one of the largest — Rithet's Bog — a 42-hectare nature sanctuary and valuable wetland for all kinds of critters.

Riding back along this rectangular route you follow the east side of the Blenkinsop Valley (unless you take the alternative route back, in which case you'll ride straight down its middle).

The valley has long been regarded as prime habitat for waterfowl, marsh birds, raptors and migratory birds. Despite there being some loss of habitat in the valley over the years i.e. tree clearing, water draining and urban development, it is still a favourite spot for birders and, because of the reconstructed 280-metre Blenkinsop Trestle, of cyclists and walkers using the Lochside Trail that runs the length of the valley.

General description

This ride begins along one of the city's most pleasant thoroughfares and carries on through two of the area's most attractive neighbour-hoods — Gordon Head and Broadmead. You'll also ride along the borders of Mount Douglas Park

and the length of the pastoral Blenkinsop Valley.

Location   Beacon Hill Park, Victoria and Saanich.

Length   33 kilometres.

Level   Moderate.

Start   Beacon Hill Park's carpark adjacent to the Children's Farm on Circle Drive.

Highlights   The tree-lined boulevard of Cook Street and its village; Mount Douglas Park; Broadmead and Rithet's Bog; farmland along Blenkinsop Road.

How to get there   Take Douglas Street southward toward Mile "0" in Beacon Hill Park. A hundred or so metres before Mile "0" turn **L** into the park on Circle Drive. The parking area is another 100 meters on the **R** before the Children's Farm.

THE RIDE

①		From the carpark adjacent to the park's Children's Farm turn **R** onto Circle Drive.
②	(0.5 km)	Turn **L** onto Dallas Road.
③	(0.9 km)	At the end of the park's northeast side turn **L** onto Cook Street. You'll stay on Cook for the next four kilometres. It's a wide boulevard with lots of trees for the first two kilometres — very safe for cyclists.
④	(5.0 km)	You've just crossed Hillside Avenue and keeping to the **R** bear **R** at the top of a short hill onto Cedar Hill Road. Follow this road for the next 5.8 kilometres.
⑤	(8.3 km)	The University Heights Shopping Mall on **R**.

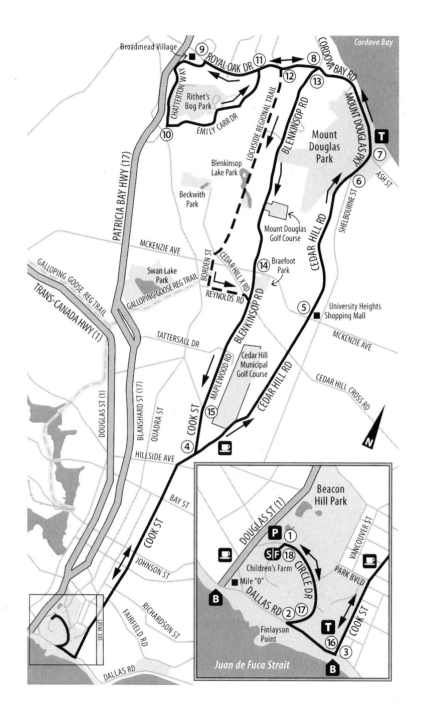

Broadmead Village

Cordova Bay

⑨ ROYAL OAK DR ⑪

CHATTERTON WAY

Rithet's Bog Park

⑩ EMILY CARR DR

LOCHSIDE REGIONAL TRAIL

⑫

⑧

CORDOVA BAY RD

⑬

BLENKINSOP RD

Mount Douglas Park

MOUNT DOUGLAS PKY

T

⑦

ASH ST

SHELBOURNE ST

⑥

Blenkinsop Lake Park

Beckwith Park

PATRICIA BAY HWY (17)

MCKENZIE AVE

Swan Lake Park

GALLOPING GOOSE REG TRAIL

TRANS-CANADA HWY (1)

GALLOPING GOOSE REG TRAIL

BORDEN ST

CEDAR HILL X RD

REYNOLDS RD

Mount Douglas Golf Course

⑭ Braefoot Park

CEDAR HILL RD

⑤ University Heights Shopping Mall

MCKENZIE AVE

TATTERSALL DR

BLENKINSOP RD

CEDAR HILL CROSS RD

DOUGLAS ST (1)

BLANSHARD ST (17)

QUADRA ST

COOK ST

MAPLEWOOD RD

Cedar Hill Municipal Golf Course

CEDAR HILL RD

⑮

④ HILLSIDE AVE ▣

BAY ST

COOK ST

JOHNSON ST

RICHARDSON ST

FAIRFIELD RD

DALLAS RD

SEE INSET

N

Beacon Hill Park

DOUGLAS ST (1)

P ①

▣

S F ⑱

Children's Farm

■ Mile "0"

CIRCLE DR

VANCOUVER ST

PARK BVLD

▣

B

DALLAS RD

② ⑰

Finlayson Point

T

⑯

COOK ST

③

B

Juan de Fuca Strait

⑥	(10.8 km)	Turn **L** onto Shelbourne Street. Shelbourne soon becomes Mount Douglas Parkway (aka Cordova Bay Road). Mount Douglas Park begins here.
⑦	(11.5 km)	The entrance to Mount Douglas Park carpark is on the **R**.
⑧	(13.4 km)	Cross the lighted junction of Blenkinsop Road and Cordova Bay Road onto Royal Oak Drive.
⑨	(15.5 km)	About 100 metres before the entrance to the Broadmead Village Shopping Centre turn **L** onto Chatterton Way. After a long downhill you'll see Rithet's Bog on your **L**.
⑩	(17.3 km)	Turn **L** at the traffic light onto Emily Carr Drive. This roadway will take you into the heart of Broadmead — a well-designed and maintained suburb.
⑪	(19.5 km)	Turn **R** onto Royal Oak Drive. (You're now on the return journey.)
⑫	(20.0 km)	Traffic lights at Lochside Drive. (**Alternate Route** [see below] on a portion of the Lochside Trail.)
⑬	(20.6 km)	At the traffic lights turn **R** onto Blenkinsop Road.
⑭	(24.3 km)	Cross McKenzie Avenue. (Red Barn grocery is on the **R**.) Blenkinsop becomes Maplewood a kilometre further on.
⑮	(26.8 km)	Bear **L** as Maplewood intersects Cook Street onto Cook. Return back to the park along Cook.
⑯	(31.8 km)	Turn **R** onto Dallas Road.
⑰	(32.1 km)	Turn **R** onto Circle Drive.
⑱	(32.7 km)	Turn **L** into carpark.

Alternate Route at ⑫

At the traffic light on Royal Oak Drive (Lochside Elementary School is on the far **R** corner) turn **R** onto Lochside Drive. This quickly becomes the gravel bed of the Lochside Trail. Continue on the trail and then, a few hundred metres past the Blenkinsop trestle, you eventually come to the junction of McKenzie Avenue. Continue across McKenzie taking Borden Street. (*Do not follow the trail signs*.) At the top of Borden turn **L** onto Reynolds Road. As Reynolds intersects Cedar Hill Cross Road turn **R** and then **R** again at the lighted intersection onto Blenkinsop Road. You are now on the route back to Beacon Hill Park. Go to ⑮. There's no appreciable difference in distance between this alterative route and the described route.

6

OAK BAY / UVIC / TEN MILE POINT

What you see as you ride through three of Victoria's most select neighbourhoods belies what is a rather beguiling history. The municipality of Oak Bay was, at the turn of the 1900s, essentially a weekend seaside resort, with a large hotel and a few summer cottages surrounded by farmland. Roughly where this ride begins is where the hotel was situated. (Actually at the corner of Windsor Road and Beach Drive.) Named Mount Baker Hotel, it was successful from its opening in 1883 and early on was able to boast visits by British royalty and the English writer Rudyard Kipling.

It wasn't long however, before developers saw the potential of the location and began buying parcels of the farmland. To attract "a good class of residents" they kept land prices high and initially it was only Victoria's wealthy that were able to buy land and build

large houses. Francis Rattenbury, the eccentric architect who had designed many of Victoria's landmarks such as the parliament buildings and the Empress Hotel, built a substantial house on Beach Drive. He called the place "Iechineel" meaning in the local First Nation's tongue "a place where good things happened." It's now a private school and you'll pass it on your return route.

Ten Mile Point (so named because it is ten nautical miles from Esquimalt Harbour) had, on its north-east side below Minnie Mountain, a dynamite manufactory plant. Built at Telegraph Cove in 1895 by the Giant Powder Company, the plant serviced the mining and road construction industries of the mainland. There are no traces of the site left although you'll ride close by on Telegraph Bay Road.

The opulent Uplands neighbourhood was once a large

180-hectare farm owned by the Hudson's Bay Company. It was the Uplands Farm which the Company sold in 1907. The land eventually landed in the hands of the Companie Franco-Canadienne which, in 1911, developed it into an exclusive suburb called simply Uplands. Divided into roughly half-hectare lots, houses were to have a minimum price of $5,000.00 and no multi-family or commercial buildings were allowed. The wide, curving roadways, the grand houses and gardens and the underground wiring and ornate street lights are the legacy that we can appreciate as we ride our modern bikes through a slice of history.

Summer outing.

General description This ride will take you through some of the area's most pleasant neighbour-hoods. You'll see part of the university, ride to the top of Ten Mile Point's Minnie Mountain and get a good look at Oak Bay and the Uplands.

Location Oak Bay's shoreline and the southern reaches of Saanich municipality.

Length 24 kilometres.

Level Moderate.

Start Oak Bay Marina's carpark.

Highlights Oak Bay Village; University of Victoria; Ten Mile Point and its Phyllis Park lookout; Queenswood Drive; Cadboro Bay Village and the Uplands.

How to get there From the intersection of Blanshard and Fort Streets turn onto the one-way Fort Street going east. After two kilometres turn **R** onto Oak Bay Avenue. Continue on this road past Oak Bay Village bearing right onto Newport Avenue. At the first intersection (intermittent light) turn **L** onto Windsor Road and then immediately **R** onto Beach Drive. Turn **L** into the Oak Bay Marina carpark after 100 metres.

How's that for a front pannier?

THE RIDE

① From the marina's carpark turn **R** onto Beach Drive. After 100 metres turn **L** onto Windsor Road.

② (1.3 km) Turn **R** onto Hampshire Road. At the village turn **R** onto Oak Bay Avenue then immediately **L** to continue along Hampshire. Cross Cranmore and Bowker after which the road becomes Musgrave Street.

③ (3.2 km) At a three-way junction in Estevan Village turn **L** onto Thompson Avenue.

④ (3.7 km) Turn **R** at the stop sign onto Cadboro Bay Road.

⑤ (4.2 km) Turn **L** at the traffic light onto Lansdowne Road turning **R** 500 metres later onto Henderson Road. After a few hundred metres you yield as Foul Bay Road joins Henderson from the **L**. You then cross Cedar Hill Cross Road and enter the University of Victoria campus. Follow the ring road to Finnerty Road (The Student Union Building is on the corner.)

⑥	(7.4 km)	Turn **R** onto Finnerty then, at the traffic light, turn **R** again onto Sinclair Road.
⑦	(8.7 km)	At the bottom of the steep downhill turn **L** onto Cadboro Bay Road at the village. Continue on Cadboro Bay Road for another kilometre.
⑧	(9.7 km)	Turn **R** into Ten Mile Point on Seaview Road. Keeping **R**, following Seaview until it joins Tudor Avenue.
⑨	(11.4 km)	Turn **R** onto Tudor Avenue.
⑩	(11.6 km)	Turn **R** onto McAnally Road which curves at a beach access to become Smuggler's Cove Road. At its end turn **L** onto Baynes Road.
⑪	(12.6 km)	Turn **R** back onto Tudor then swing **L** onto the steep uphill of Phyllis Street. At the top of Phyllis pass around the fire gate onto Arbutus Road. You are now on top of Minnie Mountain. Turn **R** here following the circular road past Phyllis Park (on your **R**) down to meet Arbutus (again) turning **R** down the steep hill to Telegraph Bay Road.
⑫	(14.4 km)	Turn **R** onto Telegraph Bay Road then **L** 300 metres later onto Queenswood Drive.
⑬	(16.6 km)	Leave Queenswood and cross Arbutus Road onto Hobbs Street. Follow Hobbs for 400 metres turning **L** onto Penryhn Street.
⑭	(17.1 km)	Turn **R** onto Cadboro Bay Road. (You're now back in the village.) After a short climb out of the village turn **L** at the Upland's gate onto Beach Drive. You soon bear **R** to take Midland Road.
⑮	(18.8 km)	At a roundabout turn **L** onto Ripon Road. Turn **L** again onto Lansdowne Road.
⑯	(19.5 km)	Turn **R** onto Beach Drive riding the four kilometres back to the Oak Bay Marine (passing on the way Uplands Park, Cattle Point, Willows Beach and Glenlyon/Norfolk School, one of Francis Rattenbury's homes — all on your **L**).

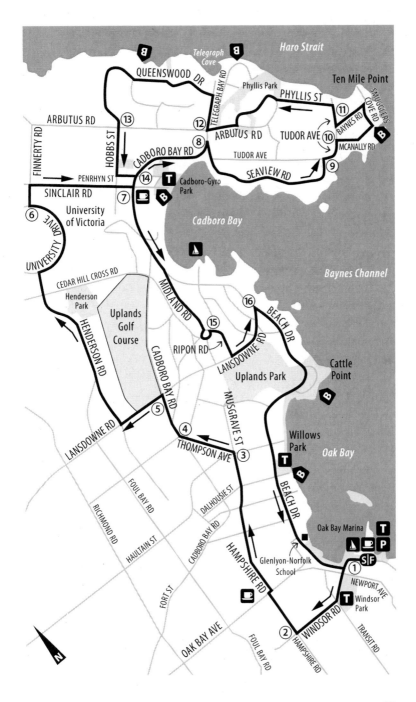

THE ARBORIST'S RIDE

Chris Paul has a passion for trees and is a keen cyclist — a pleasing and rewarding combination if you live in or around Victoria. As municipal arborist for Oak Bay he has acquired an encyclopedic knowledge of most, if not all, of the trees in the Victoria area. With this ride, Chris's arborist knowledge and his enjoyment of cycling are conjoined in a way that I hope transforms an hour or so on the bike into a lot more than just physical exercise.

The ride starts and finishes in Beacon Hill Park and follows a loop route through the leafy enclaves of Fairfield and Rockland.

Beacon Hill Park's trees are an assortment that represents Europe and Asia as well as North America. Although a few trees are centuries old, most of what we see today were planted in the late 1800s and there have been plantings ever since.

The international nature of the trees planted on the streets and roadways of the route is as varied as the park's. Perhaps the most spectacular in terms of girth and height are the giant sequoias on Moss Street and the two that serve as sentinels to Government House which were gifted to the city by the governor of California back in the 1870s. The cherry

Fairfield cherry blossoms.

and plum trees you'll see along a number of streets, though not tall, are more ostentatious. Their vivacious pink and white blooms brighten up the dreariest of spring days.

In our climate, the optimum time to ride the route is, of course, spring and early summer. But trees are for all seasons — their grace, beauty and, with some, their grandeur are to be enjoyed anytime of the year.

General description A short loop route through the city's oldest park and two picturesque neighbourhoods. As the route's name suggests, the emphasis of the ride is to enjoy the large collection of trees that are on display.

Location Victoria's Beacon Hill Park and Fairfield district.

Length 10 km

Level Easy

Start The parking lot on the west side of the park's Children's Farm.

Highlights Beacon Hill Park; sequoia trees on Moss Street; London plane trees on Chester Street; Lindsay plum on Fairfield Road and much more.

Note: Please refer to the map for a more precise location of trees identified below.

THE RIDE

① Exit the parking lot onto Circle Drive and turn **L** riding toward Douglas Street. In front of the Robbie Burns monument are two Japanese cryptomerias — the national tree of Japan. A live oak (an evergreen) is on the **R** just past the Park Way path.

② (0.2 km) Turn **R** at the giant watering can onto Douglas Street. Douglas firs line the park's border. (Over the years, these trees have provided the Great Blue Heron with a nesting habitat.)

③ (0.8 km) Opposite Michigan Street turn **R** onto the non-vehicular Bridge Way. On your **R** are two large English oaks and on the **L**, before Goodacre Lake Bridge, is an English yew.

④ (1.3 km) Continue on Bridge Way past its junction with Arbutus Way and Chestnut Row. (Guess what's down there?)

⑤ (1.6 km) After the washrooms turn **L** onto Heywood Way and then **R** onto the Douglas fir-lined Park Boulevard.

⑥ (1.9 km) Turn **L** onto Cook Street and ride through the village. Its chestnuts are some of the largest and oldest in the city.

⑦ (2.3 km) At the third crosswalk turn **R** onto Oscar Street and then first **L** onto Chester Street with its large-trunked London plane trees.

⑧ (2.6 km) As Chester meets Fairfield Road turn **R** then immediate **L** onto Trutch Street, known for its springtime blooming of Yoshino cherry trees.

⑨ (2.9 km) Turn **R** onto Richardson Street and its European birch.

⑩ (3.2 km) As you turn **L** to climb Moss Street you'll notice the tallest sequoia in Victoria at the corner of Moss and Richardson.

⑪ (3.4 km) At the stop sign turn **R** onto Rockland Avenue. You now pass more sequoia. If you're inclined (and since you'll ride past it), you might want to visit Government House. It has a formal garden with both conifer and deciduous trees in front and a large Garry oak meadow at the back.

⑫ (4.2 km) Turn **R** onto St. Charles Street and, 200 metres later, turn **L** onto Despard Avenue. Despard is lined with English oak.

⑬ (4.8 km) Turn **R** onto Gonzales Avenue. Cross Richmond Avenue and continue on Gonzales. On this street you'll find purple-leaf plum and chestnut.

⑭ (5.2 km) After crossing Richardson, you turn **R** onto Foul Bay Road. Between here and Fairfield Road the road is flanked on its **R** by London plane trees.

⑮ (5.5km) Turn **R** onto Fairfield Road. Between Richmond and

Arborist's Ride *Tree legend*

❶ Japanese cryptomeria	❻ Cherry	⑪ Kwanzan cherry
❷ Live oak	❼ White birch	⑫ Pacific madrone
❸ English oak	❽ Giant sequoia	(arbutus)
❹ English yew	❾ Purple-leaf plum	⑬ Garry oak
❺ London plane	⑩ Chestnut	⑭ Douglas fir

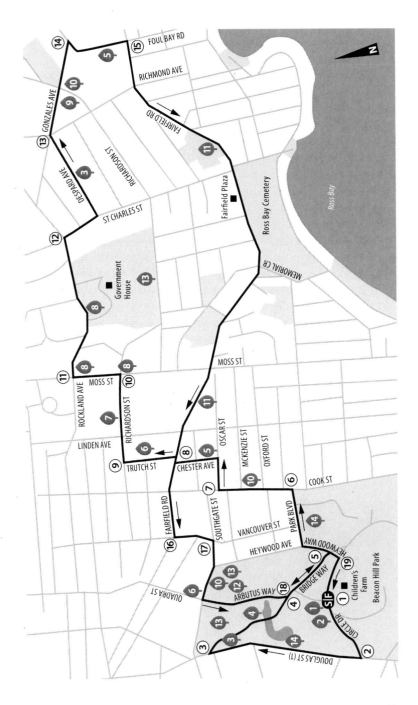

St. Charles the road is bordered with Lindsay plum (white blossoms) and Kwanzan cherry (red blossoms). On your **L** after St. Charles you'll pass Ross Bay Cemetery. Too large to describe here, it is worth a detour. The majority of its trees (pine, spruce, cedar, London plane, elm) were planted by the city in the 1930s.

⑯ (8.2 km) Having ridden along Fairfield past its second set of lights (and past more Kwanzan cherries), you turn **L** onto Vancouver Street at the following stop sign.

⑰ (8.4 km) At the stop sign turn **R** onto Southgate Street which is canopied on the **L** by large chestnuts and on the **R**, to a lesser degree, by cherry trees. After 300 metres turn **L** back into Beacon Hill Park on Arbutus Way. On the **L** on Arbutus you'll find Canada's only native broadleaf evergreen, the Pacific Madrone — usually called arbutus. On the **R** and in the field behind the arbutus are groves of Garry oaks, BC's only native oak.

⑱ (9.1 km) Turn **L** onto Bridge Way and, at the stop sign, **R** onto Heywood Way.

⑲ (9.5 km) Turn **R** onto Circle Drive riding past the Children's Farm on your **L** and, on your **R**, the best-loved tree in the park — the giant sequoia.

Goodacre Bridge, Beacon Hill Park.

ESQUIMALT / VIEW ROYAL

Once regarded as the Cinderella municipalities of the greater Victoria region, Esquimalt and View Royal comprise some of the most sought-after waterfront real estate in the area as well possessing parkland that is some of the most scenic on the south Island. Historically, Esquimalt was renowned for its harbour and farmland. In 1865, the British Navy chose Esquimalt's harbour as a permanent naval base for its Pacific fleet. In modern times the township has become known as home to Canada's Pacific Naval fleet. Almost at the same time as the Brits set up naval shop, the Hudson's Bay Company, through its subsidiary the Puget Sound Agriculture Company, established the first of four farms in the Esquimalt area. Viewfield Farm it was called, the other three: Constance Cove, Craigflower and Colwood farms followed soon after. Though no longer extant, these farms have become delightful neighbourhoods and parkland. You'll ride past or close to four of the parks: Macauley Point Park, Buxton Green Park, Saxe Point Park and the much larger Thetis Lake Park.

Disappointing as it may be, View Royal has nothing to do with royalty. The municipality's name dates back to the early 1900s when developers pitched their waterfront lots to the public by saying they had "a royal view." As you will see, they weren't far wrong especially when, after the 21 km mark, you ride down Helmcken Road to the waterfront along View Royal Avenue.

General description
Principally an urban ride, this route tours the two well-established municipalities of Esquimalt and View Royal. The short rural section is where the ride enters the large municipality of Saanich.

Location   West and South of Victoria through the neighbourhoods of Esquimalt and View Royal.

Length   31 kilometres.

Level   Easy (one steep hill).

Start   Johnson Street bridge (Blue Bridge).

Highlights   Esquimalt's waterfront and naval dockyards; access to Macauley Point Park, site of a late-19th century fort and Saxe Point Park, Thetis Lake Park and Kinsmen Gorge Park; View Royal's waterfront and beach access to Esquimalt Harbour; pubs and restaurants at Six Mile and Four Mile historic rest stops.

How to get there   Johnson Street bridge is located at the junction of Wharf, Store, Pandora and Johnson Streets on the northern edge of the downtown area. Parking is available off Store Street a few blocks from the bridge.

Esquimalt via Admirals Road.

THE RIDE

①   The ride begins at the Johnson Street bridge (the Blue Bridge) on the roadway beside the railway station and follows Esquimalt Road into the community of Esquimalt.

② (2.0 km) Turn **L** onto Dunsmuir Road.

③ (2.5 km) Turn **L** onto Head Street. The Italianate house on the **L** was built in 1893 by Captain Victor Jacobson an early settler of the area. The road bears **L** and passes the entrance to West Bay Marina.

④ (2.9 km) Turn sharp **R** onto Lyall Street and then **L** onto Peters Street. The Work Point armed forces barracks are on the **L**. For the next 1.5 km you're riding through Department of National Defense property.

⑤ (3.5 km) Turn **R** onto Bewdley Avenue.

⑥ (3.7 km) Although there is a "no-exit" sign on Anson Street turn **L** here.

⑦ (4.0 km) Turn **R** onto Munro Street. (If you continue on Anson you can access Macauley Point Park.) You pass Fleming Beach boat ramp on the **L** with the small Buxton Green Park nestled beyond.

⑧ (5.0 km) As Munro intersects Fraser Street notice on the **L** the entrance to Saxe Point Park — a small headland giving views of the ocean and the Olympic Mountains. Cross Fraser to continue on Bewdley which, after 100 m, bears **R** to become Admirals Road.

⑨ (5.4 km) Turn **L** onto Lyall Road at the stop sign and continue to the road's end.

⑩ (6.4 km) Turn sharply **R** (as if to come back on yourself) on the un-signed Esquimalt Road. You're surrounded at this point by the outer buildings of CFB Esquimalt dockyards.

⑪ (7.4 km) At the busy centre of Esquimalt turn **L** onto Admirals Road.

⑫ (10.4 km) Continue on Admirals as it crosses the Canadian Tire intersection of Craigflower Road and the Old Island Highway. You soon cross the metal bridge that separates The Gorge from Portage Inlet.

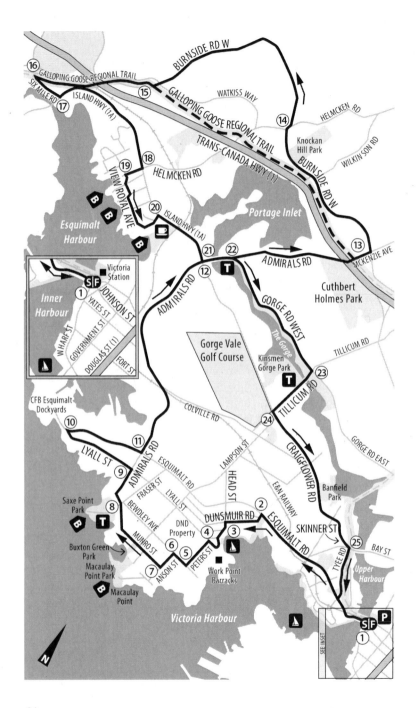

⑬	(12.2 km)	Cross the Trans-Canada Highway to McKenzie Avenue. A further 400 m turn **L** at the light-controlled junction onto Burnside Road West. (If you prefer, you can cross the highway and immediately turn **L** to take the Galloping Goose Trail that parallels the roadway. Keep on the "Goose" until ⑯.)
⑭	(14.6 km)	Cross Helmcken Road. You're now riding in rural Saanich — for a bit.
⑮	(17.3 km)	At the intersection with Watkiss Way, cross over and immediately take the Galloping Goose Trail on your **R**.
⑯	(19.0 km)	Descend off the trail at the Thetis Lake Park sign (on your **R**) and then turn **L** onto Six Mile Road. (To enter Thetis Lake Park turn **R** here. The park gates are .5 km away.)
⑰	(19.5 km)	Turn **L** at the traffic light onto the Old Island Highway. Keep **R** following the signs to View Royal.
⑱	(21.2 km)	Turn **R** onto Helmcken Road. This leads into the scenic enclave of View Royal's waterfront.
⑲	(22.0 km)	Turn **R** onto View Royal Avenue. Follow the winding avenue until it meets the Old Island Highway. (You will notice a number of beach accesses at the end of roads that dissect the avenue.)
⑳	(23.9 km)	Turn **R** onto the Old Island Highway. View Royal's town hall is located here as well as the Four Mile Restaurant and Pub.
㉑	(24.7 km)	Turn **L** onto Admirals Road. (Yes, you've been here before.)
㉒	(26.5 km)	Just past the metal bridge turn **R** onto Gorge Road West which parallels the attractive Gorge Waterway linear park.
㉓	(26.8 km)	Turn **R** onto Tillicum Road. Access to Kinsmen Gorge Park on **R** over the bridge.
㉔	(27.5 km)	Turn **L** onto Craigflower Road. This is a busy intersection but there is a filter left traffic light to help make the turn. Craigflower becomes Skinner which, in turn, becomes Tyee just before crossing Bay Street.
㉕	(30.2 km)	Turn **L** off Tyee onto Esquimalt riding the .5 km back to the Johnson Street bridge.

COASTLINE ROUTE

For a resident or visitor, it's hard not to contemplate a ride along Victoria's stunning coastline; especially on a warm summer's morning when the air is fresh and the mountains are clear as a bell and the sun's glinting on a rippling ocean. Nothing could be more grand. And the added bonuses of the ride are numerous including many viewpoints and rest stops along the way.

One might imagine that a coastal route would be flat as a pancake. Well, that's not so — as your first viewpoint will attest. It's atop King George Terrace about four kilometres into the ride. Your effort up the short but steep hill will be rewarded with a spectacular view over the Strait of Juan de Fuca to the Olympic Mountains and the San Juan Islands to the left. Immediately below is Harling Point and the Chinese Cemetery which, incidentally, was meant only as a

temporary resting place until the local Chinese community could send the deceased back to their homeland.

Oak Bay's marina is one of three spots to rest and replenish in the first part of the ride. The other two are Willows Park (and beach) and the village of Cadboro Bay. After Cadboro Bay you ride through the Queenswood Drive neighbourhood — a surprisingly tranquil and wooded road that twists amongst large homes with equally large gardens. Just before you begin the long curve of Cordova Bay you'll ride through the eastern edge of one of Victoria's favourite parks — Mount Douglas Park. The road up to the mount, fortunately, is not on this route, but the park's beach and picnic area are an option — and are very accessible.

Mattick's Farm with its stores and café is a great spot to end any bike ride. As you'll notice,

I've suggested a couple of routes back to Beacon Hill Park. You can, of course, call a taxi, or a friend, and get chauffeured back.

General description A ride along the virtually uninterrupted coastal road of Victoria's southern and eastern shoreline. You'll pass cemeteries, marinas and coffee shops. You'll ride through a golf course and one of Victoria's finest parks as well as seeing some of the best scenery the area has on view.

Location Victoria, Oak Bay, Cadboro Bay, Gordon Head and Cordova Bay.

Length
28 kilometres — one way
56 kilometres — out and back
44 kilometres — loop
Plus an alternate route back via the

Lochside Trail to the Johnson Street bridge. (An additional 13 km.)

Level Moderate.

Start Dallas Road at Beacon Hill Park's historical information sign.

Highlights Spectacular ocean views; numerous rest-stops; secluded neighbourhoods; little traffic; few crossroads except on the routes back.

How to get there From downtown take Douglas Street south (toward the ocean). Beacon Hill Park is on your **L** after the Southgate Street intersection. Bear **L** just before Douglas intersects Dallas Road (in the centre grassy area is the Mile "0" sign and the Terry Fox statue.) Continue east on Dallas for about 100 metres to the Beacon Hill historical sign on your **R**. There is ample parking along the road.

Olympic Mountains from Dallas Road.

THE RIDE

①   From the parking area along Dallas Road in front of the "Beacon Hill" historical information sign, start your trip going east along Dallas Road, i.e. away from the Douglas Street intersection. (At 2 km you'll pass Ross Bay Cemetery on your **L**.)

② (3.0 km) Turn **R** onto Ross Street. (The entrance to Gonzales Bay beach is 30 metres on the **R**.) Ross continues as Crescent Road. (3.8 km) The steep but short hill of King George Terrace begins. Trafalgar Park Lookout is at the top of the hill's crest.)

③ (4.9 km) Turn **R** onto Beach Drive (McNeill Bay begins here.) There follows a series of interesting points until ④:

- 6.3 km Victoria Golf Course
- 7.5 km Oak Bay Beach Hotel (The Snug Pub)
- 7.8 km Oak Bay Marina (café and restaurant)
- 8.9 km Glenlyon-Norfolk School (Formally Francis Rattenbury's home, "Iechineel", built in the early 1900s.)
- 9.3 km Willows Park.

④ (10.3 km) Turn **R** into Cattle Point. (This is part of the 31.25 hectare Uplands Park.)

⑤ (10.9 km) Turn **R** back onto Beach Drive. (There are numerous beach access points as you pass through this very select neighbourhood called Uplands.)

⑥ (13.0 km) At the crest of a long, gentle hill you'll pass through the Upland's gates and continue onto Cadboro Bay Road. (At 13.7 km is Cadboro Bay Village.) After a kilometre you can detour into Ten Mile Point. (See Ride #7 ⑧)

⑦ (14.7 km) Continue past a stop sign onto Telegraph Bay Road.

⑧ (15.1 km) Turn **L** onto Queenswood Drive — a thoroughly secluded road.

⑨ (16.9 km) Turn **R** onto Arbutus Road.

⑩ (17.8 km) At a stop sign turn **R** onto a continuation of Arbutus Road.

⑪ (18.9 km) Turn **R** onto Gordon Head Road. (At 19.3 km Gordon Head Road bears **L** and becomes Ferndale Road.)

⑫	(19.8 km)	Turn **R** to continue on Ferndale, then **L** on Tyndall.
⑬	(21.0 km)	Turn **R** onto Ash Road.
⑭	(22.7 km)	Turn **R** onto Cordova Bay Road (aka Mount Douglas Parkway) to ride through the wooded thoroughfare on the eastern edge of Mount Douglas Park. (The entrance to the park's beach and picnic area is at this junction.)
⑮	(24.6 km)	Turn **R** at the 4-way traffic lights onto a continuation of Cordova Bay Road.
⑯	(28.0 km)	Turn **R** into the carpark of Mattick's Farm shopping area. You'll find a grocery store, café and gift shops galore here. (At this point you can call it a day and arrange to get picked up or you can retrace your route back to Beacon Hill Park or you can continue with the following described route.)
⑰		From the entrance to Mattick's Farm cross Cordova Bay Road (with caution) and take Lochside Drive directly opposite. (This is part of the Lochside Trail.)
⑱	(30.8 km)	Continue straight on the short paved section of the Lochside Trail. (Maplegrove Road descends to your **L**.)
⑲	(30.1 km)	Continue straight on the continuation of Lochside Drive.
⑳	(31.7 km)	Turn **L** onto Royal Oak Drive. (Here there is another alternative return route. Instead of turning **L** continue straight onto the Lochside Trail following it back to its start at Johnson Street Bridge.)
㉑	(32.3 km)	Turn **R** onto Blenkinsop Road. (The Galey Farm is at 35.5 km. In the summer months, there are also numerous small roadside veggie and flower stalls.)
㉒	(36.0 km)	Cross McKenzie Avenue. (Traffic lights)
㉓	(36.6 km)	Cross Cedar Hill Cross Road. (Traffic lights)
㉔	(38.5 km)	Turn **L** at the traffic lights onto Cook Street. You now follow Cook Street back to Dallas Road (Cook Street Village is at 43 km)
㉕	(43.5 km)	Turn **R** onto Dallas Road riding back to your start.

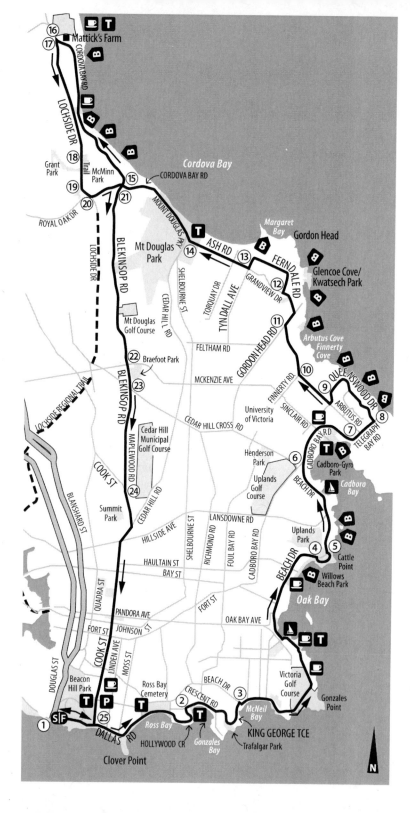

10

CIRCLE VICTORIA

As the name of this ride implies, the route describes a large circle around the city. Set on the rocky shores of a peninsula that juts into the confluence of two large bodies of water — the Strait of Juan de Fuca and Haro Strait — Victoria and its most famous (and oldest) park — Beacon Hill Park — is the ideal place to start and end a grand circle of the neighbourhoods that comprise Greater Victoria.

Because of its stunning location, Beacon Hill Park typifies for many residents and visitors the exceptional quality of life Victoria has to offer. From its formal gardens, its windswept Garry oaks, its totem pole and its two kilometre-long cliff-top walkway plus the magnificent views south over the ocean to the mountains of the Olympic Peninsula, the park seems to have everything.

On the ride you follow the Victoria shoreline going east. You pass Ross Bay Cemetery and, after Crescent, you enter Oak Bay along its scenic Beach Drive. The ride down the hill into Cadboro Bay Village is your entry into the municipality of Saanich (the largest on the island). Next is the Gordon Head neighbourhood and after riding along the eastern edge of the forested Mount Douglas Park you enter Broadmead — a large, carefully-planned community.

You cross the Pat Bay Highway to head southwest along Wilkinson Road and then, after passing the Victoria General Hospital on your left, you cross the Trans-Canada Highway and ride through the streets of View Royal. The dockyards of the Naden Naval Base are next — a signal that you're now in the municipality of Esquimalt. Because of its favourable harbour, the British Navy when they saw it in 1865, decided to make Esquimalt the permanent naval base for its Pacific fleet. It's now, of course, solely Canadian.

A favourite ocean-side park is Esquimalt's Saxe Point Park. Named for Queen Victoria's consort, Prince Albert, whose family name was Saxe-Colburg, the park is just one of three municipal parks along this jagged shoreline.

Your entry back into the city of Victoria proper is via the Inner Harbour surrounded on two sides by the grand architecture of the Victoria era — the Empress Hotel and the legislative buildings, both designed by the eccentric British architect Francis Rattenbury. Although the charm and grandeur of these buildings is a hard act to follow, your finish in Beacon Hill Park will reassure you that Mother Nature (with a little help) has the last word.

General description A loop route that takes you from the rocky shores of Beacon Hill Park to visit Oak Bay, Cadboro Bay, Cordova Bay, View Royal, Esquimalt Harbour and Victoria's Inner Harbour.

Location The municipalities of Victoria, Oak Bay, Saanich, View Royal and Esquimalt.

Length 47 kilometres.

Level Easy to moderate.

Start On Dallas Road in Beacon Hill Park a 100 metres before the intersection with Cook Street.

Highlights Beacon Hill Park; Oak Bay Marina; Cadboro Bay Village; Mount Douglas Park; Saxe Point Park; Victoria's Inner Harbour and James Bay's Ogden Point.

How to get there Follow Douglas Street south toward the ocean and Mile "0." Turn **L** onto Dallas Road. Park on the **R** opposite the totem pole 100 metres before the Cook Street intersection.

The Urban Rider.

THE RIDE

①   From the Dallas Road parking area ride east passing Clover Point **R** and Ross Bay Cemetery **L**. Dallas becomes Hollywood Crescent. After 2.8 km turn **R** off Hollywood onto Crescent Road which soon bears **L** to become the steep King George Terrace.

② (4.5 km)   Turn **R** at the bottom of King George Terrace onto Beach Drive. You continue on Beach passing Oak Bay Marina and on through the select neighbourhood of the Uplands.

③ (12.4 km) At the northern gates of the Uplands continue on what is now Cadboro Bay Road. Ride through the village as the road winds towards Ten Mile Point.

④ (14.1 km) Turn **L** onto Arbutus Road at a four-way stop.

⑤ (15.9 km) Turn **R** at a three-way stop onto a continuation of Arbutus.

⑥ (17.0 km) Turn **R** onto Gordon Head Road. (At a sharp **L** bend Gordon Head becomes Ferndale which, in turn, becomes Grandview Drive as Ferndale does a 90° **R** turn. Stay on Grandview which becomes Ash Road at the next four-way stop. Continue on Ash until it intersects Cordova Bay Road.

⑦ (20.3 km) Turn **R** onto Cordova Bay Road (aka Mount Douglas Parkway). The entrance to Mount Douglas Park's carpark/picnic area is just past this junction on the **R**.

⑧ (22.7 km) At the four-way traffic light continue straight onto Royal Oak Drive.

⑨ (25.1 km) With the Broadmead Village Shopping Centre on the **L** cross the Pat Bay Highway on the overpass. Continue through three lighted intersections onto Wilkinson Road (at the West Saanich Road intersection). Wilkinson eventually becomes Helmcken Road shortly after its intersection with Interurban Road. At 31 km you'll cross the Trans-Canada Highway and continue on a narrower but safe section of Helmcken Road.

⑩ (32.3 km) At the next light turn **L** onto the Old Island Highway.

⑪ (33.8 km) Turn **R** onto Admirals Road. (Admirals Walk Shopping Centre is on the **R**.)

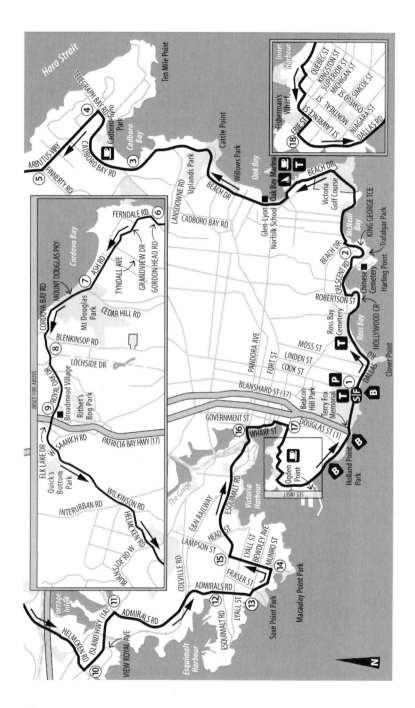

Haro Strait

Ten Mile Point

Telegraph Bay Rd

④

Cadboro Bay Rd

⑤

Arbutus Way

Finnerty Rd

Cadboro Bay Park

③

Cadboro Bay

Cattle Point

Willows Park

Lansdowne Rd

Uplands Park

Oak Bay

Oak Bay Marina

Beach Dr

Beach Dr

Victoria Golf Course

Cadboro Bay Rd

Glen-Lyon Norfolk School

McNeill Bay

King George Tce

Trafalgar Park

Harling Point

②

Beach Dr

Crescent Rd

Chinese Cemetery

Robertson St

Clover Point

Ross Bay Cemetery

Ross Bay

Hollywood Cr

Ferndale Rd

⑥

Cordova Bay

Ash Rd

Grandview Dr

Gordon Head Rd

Tyndall Ave

Mount Douglas Pky

⑦

Cordova Bay Rd

Mt Douglas Park

Cedar Hill Rd

Blenkinsop Rd

⑧

Lochside Dr

Royal Oak Dr

Broadmead Village

Rithet's Bog Park

⑨

Elk Lake Dr

Quick's Bottom Park

W Saanich Rd

Patricia Bay Hwy (17)

Interurban Rd

Wilkinson Rd

Helmcken Rd

Burnside Rd W

Moss St

Linden St

Cook St

Fort St

Pandora Ave

Blanshard St (17)

Beacon Hill Park

Terry Fox Memorial

Dallas Rd

①

Government St

⑯

Wharf St

⑰

Douglas St (1)

Ogden Point

Holland Point Park

Victoria Harbour

The Gorge

Esquimalt Rd

E&N Railway

Head St

Lampson St

⑮

Lyall St

Bewdley Ave

Munro St

⑭

Fraser St

Colville Rd

Admirals Rd

⑫

Lyall St

⑬

Saxe Point Park

Macaulay Point Park

Esquimalt Rd

Esquimalt Harbour

Portage Inlet

⑪

Admirals Rd

Island Hwy (1A)

View Royal Ave

Helmcken Rd

⑩

INSET FOR ABOVE

SEE INSET

N

Inner Harbour

Fisherman's Wharf

⑱

Quebec St

Kingston St

Superior St

Michigan St

St Lawrence St

Montreal St

Oswego St

Simcoe St

Niagara St

Erie St

Dallas Rd

44

⑫ (36.7 km) After passing the Naden Naval Base on the **R** you cross Esquimalt Road at the town's centre continuing on Admirals.

⑬ (37.7 km) Turn briefly onto Bewdley (the entrance to Saxe Point Park is a few metres on the **R**) crossing Fraser Street onto Munro Street.

⑭ (38.1 km) Passing the Fleming Beach boat launch and Buxton Green Park on your **R** turn **L** onto Lampson Street.

⑮ (39.0 km) Turn **R** onto Esquimalt Road. You'll ride on this road back into Victoria. (Take care travelling on the metal-grated surface of the Johnson Street bridge.)

⑯ (42.0 km) Just over the Johnson Street bridge turn **R** onto Wharf Street.

⑰ (42.7 km) Turn **R** onto Government Street at the art deco Victoria Tourism building and then, after passing in front of the Empress Hotel turn **R** onto Belleville Street. (The BC Legislative Building is on your **L**.)

⑱ You now encounter a series of short streets that follows the coastline. You'll pass Fisherman's Wharf (44 km) and, as you join Dallas Road, the cruise ship terminal, café and the Ogden Point breakwater are all on your **R**. Continue on Dallas back to Beacon Hill Park and your starting point.

Early morning ride along Victoria's waterfront.

Saanich, Central Saanich, North Saanich and Sidney

ELK/BEAVER LAKE / BRENTWOOD BAY / SAANICHTON

Starting on the shores of one of Victoria's most extensively used parks — Elk/Beaver Lake Regional Park, this circular route takes you through countryside that typifies the charm and attraction of the Saanich Peninsula. You'll come across a myriad hobby farms, farmers markets, country roads and, of course, the "big one", the entrance road to the renowned Butchart Gardens. You'll also brush the small communities of Brentwood Bay and Saanichton. At almost 24 kilometres, this compact circle will be a very pleasing afternoon's outing. And, if you're in the mood, you can take a dip in the safe waters of Hamsterly Beach followed by a lazy picnic under one of the wide-boughed weeping willows of the park's spacious lawn.

General description After following the northern extremity of Elk/Beaver Lake Regional Park this ride follows a circular loop through some of the area's most picturesque countyside. A major side-trip would be to the famous Butchart Gardens about halfway through the ride. (Add another three days to your trip!)

Location The municipalities of Saanich and Central Saanich, 12 kilometres from Victoria's downtown.

Length 24 kilometres.

Level   Easy to moderate.

Start   Hamsterly Beach carpark at the northeast end of Elk/Beaver Lake Park.

Highlights   Elk/Beaver Lake Regional Park's Hamsterly Beach; rural roads; road-side fruit, veggie and flower stalls.

How to get there   Follow Blanshard Street/Pat Bay Highway (#17) out of town. After about 12 kilometres turn **L** at the traffic light onto Sayward Road. (There are two gas stations at this intersection on your **L**.) Follow Sayward as it quickly turns **L** onto Hamsterly Road. Then another quick **R** turn brings you onto Brookleigh Road. The entrance to Elk/Beaver Park's Hamsterly Beach is 50 metres on the **L**.

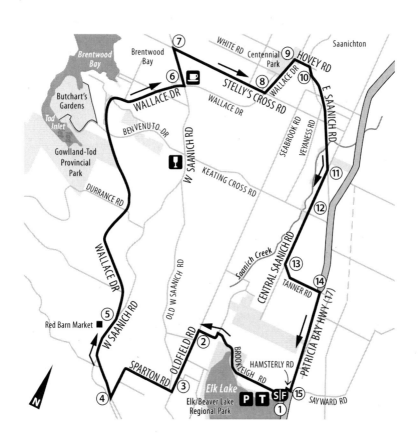

THE RIDE

①   From the park's Hamsterly Beach carpark turn **L** onto Brookleigh Road.

② (2.3 km)   Turn **L** onto Oldfield Road.

③ (3.6 km)   Turn **R** onto Sparton Road. This is a short but hilly road — mercifully, mostly down.

④ (5.2 km)   Turn **R** onto West Saanich Road.

⑤ (6.7 km)   Just after the Red Barn Market (on the **L**) turn **L** onto Wallace Drive. At 10.5 km you cross Benvenuto Avenue (which ends at Butchart Gardens) and continue on to Brentwood Bay Village.

⑥ (12.7 km)   Turn **L** at the major intersection onto West Saanich Road climbing the hill to Stelly's Cross Road.

⑦ (13.5 km)   Turn right onto Stelly's Cross Road just after you've crested the hill.

⑧ (15.5 km)   Turn **L** onto Wallace Drive. You'll pass Centennial Park on your **L**.

⑨ (16.2 km)   Opposite the park's main entrance turn **R** onto Hovey Road — a short road that leads to East Saanich Road.

⑩ (16.5 km)   Turn **R** onto East Saanich Road.

⑪ (18.5 km)   Turn **R** onto Central Saanich Road just before a large sign indicating the route to the Pat Bay Highway.

⑫ (19.4 km)   Cross Keating Cross Road.

⑬ (20.3 km)   Bear **L** onto Tanner Road. Central Saanich Road continues straight to end at Bear Hill Regional Park.

⑭ (21.3 km)   Turn **R** onto the Pat Bay Highway. There is a good shoulder here and it's only a short ride back to Elk/Beaver Lake park.

⑮ (23.3 km)   Turn **R** at the traffic light onto Sayward Road, then sharp **L** and then **R** before turning into the carpark at Hamsterly Beach.

ELK /BEAVER LAKE /
CORDOVA BAY

Elk/Beaver Lake has a long history, relatively speaking. Once two separate lakes, Elk and Beaver Lakes were joined when, in the late 1800s, Colquitz Creek was dammed to enlarge one of Greater Victoria's main sources of water. Story has it that around that time, Victoria's residents found small fish and tadpoles coming through their taps. To rectify the problem filter beds were constructed in 1896. Apparently, they produced the right effect. The ride has its start at the carpark that lies atop the beds.

The five kilometre trail that parallels the lake on its west side (and the one you'll ride on) was, from 1894 until 1919, a railway line. Known as the "Cordwood Limited" it was part of the Victoria and Sidney Railway and was regarded by many who travelled that portion as its most

scenic but most dangerous. After the railway's demise, the lake became popular as Victoria's "Freshwater Playground." In the 1930s the lakeshore accommodated a tea-room, a chocolate factory and an outdoor dance hall. Since becoming a regional park in 1966, there is essentially no commercial activity within its confines and is now known for the great variety of activities that people participate in, on and around the lake, from rowing to running; from horseback riding to fishing.

General description A loop route that takes you along the western shore of Elk Lake, down the slope to Cordova Bay, then back along a paved portion of the Lochside Trail and on through Broadmead.

Location Ten kilometres north of Victoria in the municipality of Saanich.

Length   18 kilometres.

Level   Easy.

Start   Beaver Lake Park: second parking lot.

Highlights   Views over Elk Lake; Mattick's Farm's stores and café; views over Haro Strait along Lochside Drive; lakeside picnic.

How to get there   Take Blanshard Street out of town. The Pat(ricia) Bay Highway (#17) is the continuation of Blanshard after about 5 kilometres. Exit on Royal Oak Drive after 8 kilometres. Turn **L** on Royal Oak Drive and cross the highway. At the second traffic light turn **R** onto Elk Lake Drive. After a kilometre turn **L** into the entrance of Beaver Lake Park. Park at the second, gravelled parking lot about 800 metres from the park entrance.

Now is this the right way?

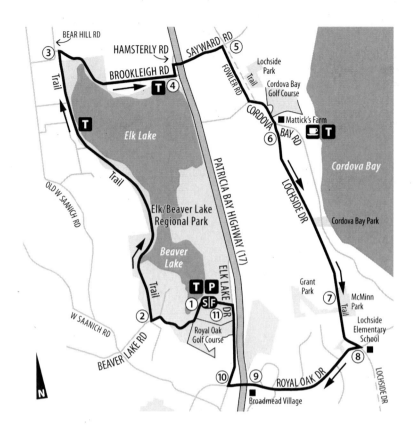

THE RIDE

(1)   From the park's carpark area turn **R** riding out of the park on Beaver Lake Road.

(2)   (0.5 km)   Just after the park entrance to the equestrian centre turn **R** onto a wide, straight trail that takes you along the western shore of the lake to the Bear Hill Road exit.

(3)   (6.0 km)   Turn **R** at the park gates onto Brookleigh Road.

(4)   (8.0 km)   Turn **L** as Brookleigh intersects Hamsterly Road (Hamsterly Beach is on your **R**) onto Hamsterly and **R** onto Sayward Road. Cross the Pat Bay Highway riding down Sayward.

(5)   (9.8 km)   Bear **R** at the bottom of the hill as Sayward becomes Fowler Road.

⑥	(10.1 km)	With Mattick's Farm shopping area on your **L** turn **R** onto Lochside Drive. (This is part of the Lochside Trail.)
⑦	(12.5 km)	Continue straight on the short paved section of the Lochside Trail. (Maplegrove descends to your **L**.)
⑧	(13.5 km)	Turn **R** onto Royal Oak Drive at the traffic light.
⑨	(15.0 km)	Cross the Pat Bay Highway via the overpass.
⑩	(15.3 km)	At the second set of lights after the overpass turn **R** onto Elk Lake Drive.
⑪	(17.0 km)	Turn **L** into the entrance of Beaver Lake Park. Ride through the first parking area to your car at the second, gravelled parking lot.

Elk Lake.

BEAVER LAKE / PROSPECT LAKE / BRENTWOOD BAY

The twist and turns of the first kilometres of the ride will set the stage for what could be one of those outings where you just want to stop and explore interesting places along the way. About two kilometres into the ride you'll come across Glendale Gardens and Woodland (formerly known as the Horticultural Centre of the Pacific) on Quayle Road. The gardens are a not-for-profit organization that was founded in 1979 to manage a large, 50-hectare piece of land of which about two hectares are cultivated as a teaching and demonstration garden. Fortunately, it's open to the public and its tranquil, rural environment has, along with its flourishing garden, well over 40 hectares of intentionally-undeveloped terrain that includes areas of wetland, Garry oak forest and other native plant habitats. If you stop for a visit you'll find a tearoom and

gift shop plus a library and greenhouses to poke around in.

Once you encounter Goward Road you'll wonder how on earth such a combination of human habitation and forest splendour could exist intertwined. Goward, by any standard, is one of the outstanding roads in Greater Victoria. The added attraction of this road is that it ends by the shores of Prospect Lake at Whitehead Park — a small lakeshore park very suitable for picnicking after the undulations of Goward.

As your make you way north-ward the roads flatten out (a little) and you soon cross Benvenuto Drive (the road to the famous Butchart Gardens) to enter the village of Brentwood Bay. This marks the halfway point of the ride and the cafés and pub can be tantalizing on a hot summer's day. Other diversions as you leave

53

Brentwood Bay are the interesting Butterfly Gardens and the Victoria Estate Winery, both having their entrances off Benvenuto Drive. Your ride back is principally along Old West Saanich Road which is basically a collection of hills and attractive homes and gardens. The final five kilometres is, thankfully, flat as a pancake as you enter Elk/Beaver Park and ride along the vestigial railway bed of the Victoria and Sidney Line that ran along the lake's shore between 1894 and 1919.

General description   There are some hills on this ride but they're on the scenically-pleasing rural roads of Saanich and Central Saanich. You'll finish on the very flat old railway grade that follows Elk/Beaver

Lake Park's western edge.

Location   West Saanich, Central Saanich and Brentwood Bay.

Length   29 kilometres.

Level   Moderate.

Start   Beaver Lake Park carpark.

Highlights   Glendale Gardens and Woodland; picnic area on the shores of Prospect Lake; ride through one of the area's most attractive parks.

How to get there   Take Blanshard Street (Highway #17) out of town. After 8 kilometres take the Royal Oak Drive exit. Turn left over the highway on Royal Oak Drive. After 200 metres turn **R** at the traffic light onto Elk Lake Drive. At one kilometre turn **L** into the entrance of Beaver Lake Park. Continue past the first paved parking lot to the large gravelled parking lot in front of the covered picnic area.

THE RIDE

①		Exit the carpark turning **R** to follow the park road which becomes Beaver Lake Road at the park boundary.
②	(1.3 km)	Turn **R** onto West Saanich Road then immediately **L** onto the continuation of Beaver Lake Road (West Saanich Road is busy along this stretch plus the fact that the intersection is on a bend — take care!).
③	(1.5 km)	Turn **L** onto Beaver Road.
④		Beaver Road turns sharply **R** to become Quayle Road. Glendale Gardens and Woodland is situated at this corner.

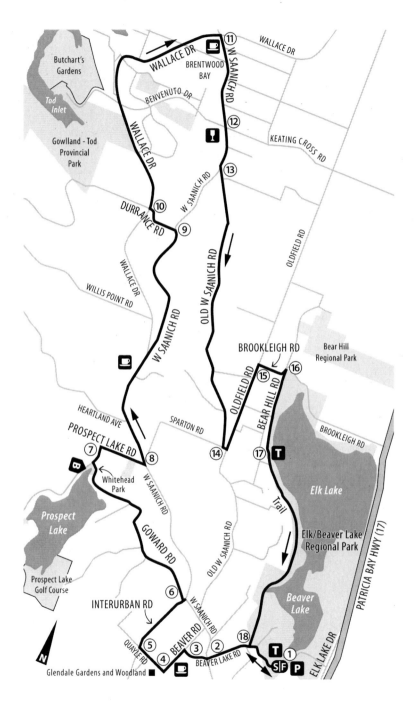

Butchart's
Gardens

Tod
Inlet

Gowlland - Tod
Provincial
Park

WALLACE DR

BRENTWOOD
BAY

⑪

W SAANICH RD

WALLACE DR

BENVENUTO DR

⑫

KEATING CROSS RD

WALLACE DR

⑬

W SAANICH RD

OLD W SAANICH RD

DURRANCE RD

⑩

⑨

WALLACE DR

WILLIS POINT RD

OLDFIELD RD

W SAANICH RD

BROOKLEIGH RD

Bear Hill
Regional Park

⑮

⑯

OLDFIELD RD

BEAR HILL RD

BROOKLEIGH RD

HEARTLAND AVE

SPARTON RD

PROSPECT LAKE RD

⑦

⑧

⑭

⑰ **T**

Whitehead
Park

W SAANICH RD

B

Elk Lake

Prospect
Lake

Trail

Elk/Beaver Lake
Regional Park

GOWARD RD

OLD W SAANICH RD

Prospect Lake
Golf Course

⑥

INTERURBAN RD

Beaver
Lake

PATRICIA BAY HWY (17)

W SAANICH RD

⑤

④

③

②

⑱

T ①

QUAYLE RD

BEAVER RD

BEAVER LAKE RD

S **F** **P**

ELK LAKE DR

N

Glendale Gardens and Woodland ■

55

⑤	(2.5 km)	Turn **R** onto Interurban Road. There is a bike lane along this section of road.
⑥	(3.5 km)	Just before Interurban intersects West Saanich Road, turn **L** onto Goward Road. Goward is both hilly and twisting — watch for traffic.
⑦	(6.0 km)	Turn **R** onto Prospect Lake Road. Whitehead Park is situated here, on the **L** at the head of Prospect Lake. There is beach access and a picnic area.
⑧	(7.0 km)	Turn **L** onto West Saanich Road. After 1.2 km you'll pass the Red Barn Market on your **L**. A bike lane begins here as the road rises.
⑨	(10.5 km)	Turn **L** down the steep descent of Durrance Road (opposite the Lion of Judah Ministry Centre).
⑩	(11.4 km)	Turn **L** at the bottom of the hill onto Wallace Drive. You'll cross Benvenuto Avenue (which ends at Butchart Gardens) and then ride into the heart of Brentwood Bay Village.
⑪	(15.0 km)	Turn **R** at the main intersection onto West Saanich Road. There are a number of amenities here including stores, pub and coffee shop.
⑫	(16.5 km)	Cross this traffic lighted main intersection. Butterfly Gardens and Victoria Estate Winery are on the right-hand side. (Both have entrances on Benvenuto Avenue)
⑬	(17.0 km)	Turn **L** onto Old West Saanich Road. (You will be crossing oncoming traffic on a slight up-hill on a bend so take care.) Old West Saanich Road is a scenic delight but there's a price — lots of hills.
⑭	(21.0 km)	At the five-way junction turn **L** onto Oldfield Road.
⑮	(22.3 km)	Turn **R** at Brookleigh Road.
⑯	(22.8 km)	Half a kilometre along Brookleigh turn abruptly **R** onto Bear Hill Road — the paved entrance road to Elk/Beaver Lake Regional Park.
⑰	(23.6 km)	Bear Hill Road now becomes a broad trail (a vestigial railway bed). Follow this trail for another 5 kilometres until it ends at Beaver Lake Road.
⑱	(28.5 km)	Turn **L** and ride the .5 kilometres back to your starting point.

TILLICUM MALL / INTERURBAN ROAD / HIGHLAND ROAD

You know how some rides are often defined by something distinctive. It could be an interesting section of road, an old building en route, a beautiful vista or even a brutally steep hill. Well, the defining features of this ride are a little more subtle and are twofold. One, you get to explore an area that not too many people know about. Nestled between Interurban Road and Prospect Lake Road is a large rural area that has few roads and even fewer houses. Conway and Hector Roads were once part of an early 1900s subdivision called Burnside Park and although the roads are winding and a little hilly, they provide the perfect environment for small hobby farms, large gardens, raising horses and the odd cow or llama.

There are a couple of parks in the area also. Logan Park is the oldest of the two having been established in 1925 and named after the man who once owned the property, Edward Logan. The other is Trevlac Park, quirkily named after Giff Calvert who had once developed the property into a private wildlife preserve. Trevlac is Calvert spelt backwards.

The second feature (also little known) is a short stretch of gravel fire-road that connects Munn Road to Thetis Lake Park's Highland Road entrance. It's all downhill and leads you through the beautiful forest land that borders the park.

General description Despite the ride's start at a shopping mall, it explores some of the area's best-kept, semi-rural secrets. Expect some hills (of course) and the surprise of a 3.2 kilometre section of gravel.

Location South-west Saanich, View Royal, Thetis Lake Park.

Length 30 kilometres.

Level Moderate to strenuous.

Start Tillicum Mall carpark.

Highlights The pastoral quality of Conway, Hector and Charlton Roads; riding through the coniferous forest of Francis/King and Thetis Lake parks; possible picnic by the shores of Thetis Lake.

How to get there Take Douglas Street (Trans-Canada Highway) going north. After about 2 kilometres turn **L** onto Burnside Road East. A further 2 plus kilometres turn **L** into the carpark of Tillicum Mall. Park on the **R** where two restaurants are located.

If you prefer to ride to the start of this route from town, access the Galloping Goose Trail at its Johnson Street trailhead. Between the 5 and 6 kilometre signs take the off ramp (just before the first trestle bridge) down to the **R**. This leads to the junction of Burnside Road West and Interurban Road. Turn **R** onto Interurban. At this point you are 300 metres into the ride. (Adjust your computer accordingly.)

"We can go after the next one."

THE RIDE

① Exit the Tillicum Mall carpark turning **L** onto Burnside Road West. After passing under the Trans-Canada Highway the road becomes Interurban Road. There is a good bike lane the whole length of this road. You'll pass Panama Flats, pond and hill just after 2 kilometres on your **R** and then, at 4.3 kilometres, the entrance to Camosun College.

② (4.9 km) Just past the college campus turn **L** onto the narrow, hilly Conway Road.

③ (5.8 km) At a sharp **R** bend Conway becomes Hector Road. Continue on Hector until it makes a full circle to arrive back at Interurban. (Logan and Trevlac Parks are at 5.9 and 6.8 kilometres respectively.)

④ (8.6 km) Turn **R** onto Interurban Road.

⑤ (9.5 km) After almost a kilometre turn **R** onto North Road.

⑥ (9.9 km) Turn **R** onto Hastings Street at the stop sign.

⑦ (10.8 km) At the end of Hastings turn **R** onto Granville Avenue.

⑧ (11.4 km) Turn **L** onto Charlton Road.

⑨ (13.2 km) Turn **R** onto Burnside Road West.

⑩ (13.4 km) Turn **R** onto Prospect Lake Road.

⑪ (14.8 km) Turn **L** onto Munn Road. (The entrance to Francis/King Park is 400 metres on the **R**.)

⑫ (17.4 km) On the **L** 300 metres past Rolla Place is the beginning of a 3.2 km fire-road leading to Highland Road and Thetis Lake Park. You'll find the opening to this gravel road by riding to the **L** of a private house #2359. The trail/road begins rather roughly as it passes under power-lines but after about 1.5 kilometres this downward, "twisty-turny" trail/road becomes a well-groomed gravel road. (There are gates at both ends of this right-of-way.)

⑬ (20.6 km) Turn **L** onto Highland Road (Barker Road goes to the **R**.) You are now within the boundaries of Thetis Lake Park. (Notice a wide trail 200 metres past McKenzie Creek Bridge on the **R**. This leads to Thetis Lake.) Highland becomes Watkiss Way about

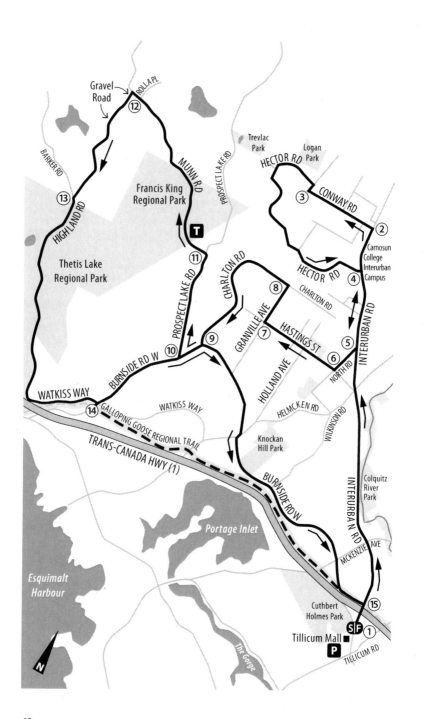

1 kilometre before the junction with Burnside Road West.

⑭   (24.2 km)   Turn **L** onto Burnside Road West at the four-way junction. You'll soon pass Prospect Lake and Charlton Roads on your **L** as you make your way back to the mall. (An alternate route to the next checkpoint is, instead of turning **L** on Burnside you cross the road and take the Galloping Goose Trail. You exit **L** off the trail just after the trestle bridge onto Interurban. Turn **L** on Interurban riding back to the mall.)

⑮   (29.6 km)   Turn **R** at the junction of Burnside Road West and Interurban Road. (If you're returning to town via the Galloping Goose Trail take the access on your **L**.)

⑯   (30.0 km)   Turn **R** into the Tillicum Mall carpark.

Looking forward to the ride.

CAREY ROAD / LAYRITZ PARK /
WEST BURNSIDE ROAD

Those of you who know the area well will recognize the abundance of small parks speckling the greater Victoria landscape. This ride goes through one and passes by six others.

Although this is one of the shorter rides in the book it has just about everything that Victoria's suburbs have to offer; except the ocean. Starting at that most ubiquitous of urban places — a shopping centre — the route travels along house-lined streets, passes farms, glances at Camosun College's Interurban campus and, as I've said, goes through a small park and skirts several others.

One of the parks' names has a particular history. Panama Hill Park derives its name from the adjacent flatland called Panama Flats. The flats were so named because they reminded an early owner of the property of the land through which the Panama Canal was being constructed. He had worked on its construction as an engineer in 1904.

The old-fashioned way.

As you can see from the map, the route is a loop with an out-and-back panhandle. Apart from Grange Road's short and steepish hill the majority of the ride is very easy on the legs.

General description A flattish loop route that has a good mixture of suburban and semi-rural landscapes to explore.

Location Just north of Victoria in the municipalities of Saanich and View Royal.

Length 20 kilometres.

Level Easy.

Start Uptown parking area off Douglas Street just before it becomes the Trans-Canada Highway.

Highlights Panama Flats; Layritz Park; rural roads and hobby farms; tree-lined Grange Road.

How to get there Take Douglas Street out of town. Just before it becomes the Trans-Canada Highway turn **R** onto Carey Road and then **R** again into the carpark of the Uptown parking area.

THE RIDE

①		From the shopping centre's north-end parking area turn **R** onto Carey Road.
②	(1.3 km)	Bear **L** at the pedestrian traffic light following the Carey Road sign.
③	(1.7 km)	Cross the four-laned McKenzie Avenue.
④	(2.5 km)	Panama Flats farmland on your **L**.
⑤	(4.3 km)	Turn **R** onto Wilkinson Road.
⑥	(4.7 km)	Turn **L** at the next traffic light onto Mann Road. The Mann Road entrance to Layritz Park is at the end of this short section of road.
⑦		Once in the park and on the signed Glendale Trail you'll turn **R** after 200 metres onto a good, wide chip trail. This curves **L** behind a baseball diamond then turns **R** into a treed section. The chip soon becomes pavement again which, in turn, runs into Markham Street.
⑧	(5.8 km)	Continue straight on Markham Street. The entrance to Vancouver Island Technology Park is on the **L**.
⑨	(6.6 km)	Turn **L** onto West Saanich Road.

⑩	(8.2 km)	Turn **L** onto Interurban Road.
⑪	(11.7 km)	After Interurban crosses Durrell Creek turn **R** onto North Road.
⑫	(12.1 km)	Turn **R** onto Hastings Street.
⑬	(13.1 km)	Turn **L** onto Granville Avenue.
⑭	(13.8 km)	Turn **L** onto Burnside Road West.
⑮	(14.6 km)	Cross Helmcken Road. (The entrance to Knockan Hill Park is at 15 km.)
⑯	(16.0 km)	Turn **L** onto Grange Road. (Spectrum High School is on the **R**.)
⑰	(17.0 km)	Turn **R** onto Interurban Road.
⑱	(17.5 km)	Turn **L** onto Marigold Road.
⑲	(18.0 km)	Turn **R** onto Carey Road. Continue on Carey until the Uptown parking area.

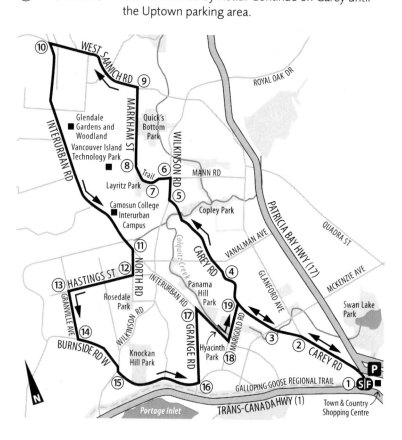

16

MOUNT DOUGLAS PARK / BLENKINSOP VALLEY

The locals know it simply as "Mt. Doug." But what they're referring to is the 182-hectare wilderness preserve properly called Mount Douglas Park. This wonderful parkland is crowned by the imposing "Mt. Doug" summit which, at 227 metres, can be seen from almost anywhere in the eastern part of Greater Victoria.

Originally called Cedar Hill or "Hill of Cedars" because the forest was the source of Fort Victoria's fencing in 1843, Mount Douglas was officially given its present name by British Columbia's first governor, Sir James Douglas back in 1858. Fortunately, despite efforts to turn the forest into farmland, Douglas recognized the significance of the land as special and beautiful and set it aside as a park.

The Blenkinsop Valley takes its name from one of the early landowners in the area. George Blenkinsop was an official with the Hudson's Bay Company and, although he never lived in the valley, saw it while he was staying at Fort Victoria. He recognized its utility as potential farmland and decided to buy it. One of the dominant features of the valley is Blenkinsop Lake. The Lake is a far smaller body of water than a century ago and its scrubby foliage a far cry from the once glorious mixed forest that surrounded it. An old inventory counted 21 Sitka Spruce — the largest being 80 feet high and four feet in diameter. Hemlock, red cedar, balsam, Douglas fir and Garry oak were also in profusion. It's an irony that the lake was once called Lost Lake — certainly much of its original splendor has been lost to modern urbanization and degradation. Still, the valley has much to offer especially as the Lochside Trail courses down its centre. Much of the land is protected as agriculture land under the province's Agricultural Land Reserve and the creek that runs part of its length has been restored over the past decades from its status as a storm drainage and sewage ditch.

General description A route that describes a modest loop around Mount Douglas Park. In doing so, it takes into its orbit the pastural Blenskinsop Valley and briefly skirts the border of Broadmead and Gordon Head suburbs.

Location Mount Douglas Park, Gordon Head, Blenkinsop Valley.

Length 10 kilometres.

Level Easy.

Start Mount Douglas Park's Churchill Drive carpark. (Additional parking on Cedar Hill Road adjacent to park).

Highlights Mount Douglas Park; the Lochside Trail as it cuts through the Blenkinsop Valley; the recently-designated Mount Douglas Parkway.

How to get there From downtown take Blanshard Street the few blocks to Fort Street. Turn **R** onto Fort then turn **L** at the fourth block onto Cook Street. Follow Cook Street for just over two kilometres and after crossing the traffic lights at the Hillside Avenue junction bear **R** at the top of a slight hill to take Cedar Hill Road. Follow this road for 10 kilometres before turning **L** at its intersection with Shelbourne Street. Once on Shelbourne you travel a few metres to turn **L** onto Churchill Drive — the entrance to Mount Douglas Park. There is space for a few cars on the **R** on Churchill. There is additional roadside parking back on Cedar Hill Road adjacent to the park.

Exiting Mt. Douglas Park.

THE RIDE

① From Mt. Doug Park's Churchill Drive carpark exit the park turning **R** onto Cedar Hill Cross Road.

② (1.8 km) Turn **R** onto Mount Douglas Cross Road.

③ (2.4 km) As Mount Douglas Cross Road turns sharply **L** cross the left of the road to joining and travel along the paved Blenkinsop Spur portion of the Saanich Centennial Trail that parallels Mount Douglas Cross Road. You'll cross Blenkinsop Road at the bottom of the hill. Keep to the trail until its junction with the Lochside Trail.

④ (3.6 km) Turn **R** onto the Lochside Trail. You immediately cross the 288 metre Blenkinsop Trestle. Continue on the trail until its intersection with Royal Oak Drive.

⑤ (6.6 km) Turn **R** onto Royal Oak Drive.

⑥ (7.2 km) At the next light cross the intersection onto the Mount Douglas Parkway (aka Cordova Bay Road). Ride the parkway for a further 2.5 kilometres back to the Churchill Drive carpark and your car.

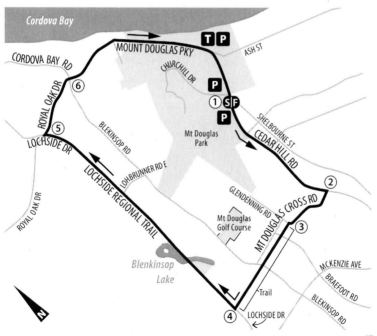

UVIC / GORDON HEAD

On this relatively short ride you'll cover a considerable amount of territory on the south-eastern edge of greater Victoria. Starting from the carpark adjacent to the delightful but miniature Henderson Park you'll ride through the centre of the university and into Gordon Head — a large promontory jutting into Haro Strait. Distinctly suburban, Gordon Head has one or two special features, the most outstanding being, in my mind, the small but spectacular Glencoe Cove/Kwatsech Park. Donated to Saanich municipality in the early nineties by the Moore family, which had owned the land since the 1940s, this park has considerable significance both as a well preserved Garry oak headland with some of the rarest plants in Canada and also as a First Nation's shell midden site indicating that it was an ancient settlement. If you're there early on a clear summer's morning, you can experience the sun gleaming on Mt. Baker's summit and perhaps sight a sailboat making its way to Roche Harbour at the northern tip of San Juan Island.

Like many of the place names on BC's coast, Gordon Head was named after a British naval officer, Captain John Gordon, who was surveying the southern coast in 1846. The first home was built four years later in 1850. Perhaps the most well-known early settlers were the farming Vantreight family. (A small park in the area bears the family name.)

The second half of the ride takes you through the wonderfully-forested Mount Doug Park (as it's known locally) and then back along the eastern side of the pastoral Blenkinsop Valley.

General description

A circular route that courses through the University of Victoria, suburban Gordon Head and Mount Douglas Park.

Location   Mainly in the south-eastern portion of the municipality of Saanich.

Length   22 kilometres.

Level   Moderate.

Start   Henderson Recreation Centre's carpark (Note: There's a three hour parking restriction between 9 am and 5 pm Monday–Friday.) Street parking is an option.

Highlights   University of

Victoria; Glencoe Cove/Kwatsech Park in Gordon Head; possible picnic in Mount Douglas Park's beach area.

How to get there   Leave downtown on Blanshard Street turning **R** onto Hillside Avenue at two kilometres. Continue on Hillside past the Hillside Mall at which point Hillside becomes Lansdowne Road. Turn **L** onto Foul Bay Road (which becomes Henderson Road) at the second set of lights after the mall. After a kilometre or so turn **R** onto Cedar Hill Cross Road at the traffic lights. The entrance to Henderson Recreation Centre is 300 metres on the **R**.

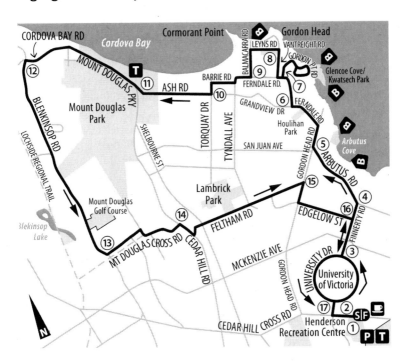

THE RIDE

① From the recreation centre's carpark turn **L** onto Cedar Hill Cross Road.

② (0.5 km) Turn **R** at the entrance to the university riding the short distance onto University Drive. (This is a one-way ring road so you'll turn **R** when you meet it.)

③ (1.6 km) Turn **R** onto Finnerty Road. The university bookstore and student union building are at this junction.

④ (2.4 km) Having crossed the lighted junction of Finnerty with McKenzie Avenue and Sinclair Road at 1.9 km, turn **L** at the three-way stop onto Arbutus Road.

⑤ (3.5 km) Turn **R** onto Gordon Head Road. At the bottom of the hill the road bears **L** to become Ferndale Road.

⑥ (4.4 km) Turn **R** onto the continuation of Ferndale.

⑦ (4.8 km) After Ferndale turns sharply **L** you take the first **R** down the out-and-back Gordon Point Drive. Glencoe Cove-Kwatsech Park is at the bottom of the hill and offers great views over the Haro Strait, Mt. Baker and the San Juan Islands. Continue round the points for about a kilometre until you intersect the drive again. Turn **L** riding up the hill back to Ferndale. Turn **R** onto Ferndale and then **R** again down Vantreight Drive.

⑧ (6.7 km) With Vantreight Park on your **L** turn **L** onto Leyns Road. At the end of Leyns turn **L** onto Balmacarra Road.

⑨ (7.5 km) At the top of Balmacarra turn **R** to rejoin Ferndale. Two hundred metres later turn **L** onto Tyndall Avenue then 50 metres later turn **R** onto Barrie Road. Barrie turns **L** to become Torquay Drive.

⑩ (8.3 km) Turn **R** at the lighted stop sign onto Ash Road.

⑪ (9.5 km) Turn **R** onto Cordova Bay Road (aka Mount Douglas Parkway). The entrance to Mount Douglas Park's beach picnic area and carpark is immediately on your **R**.

⑫ (11.5 km) Turn **L** onto Blenkinsop Road. Around the 13 km mark is the Mercer Trail entrance to Mount Douglas Park on your **L** and an access road to the Lochside Trail on your **R**.

(13) (14.8 km) Just after the Galey Farm Market on **R** turn **L** onto Mount Douglas Cross Road. (The Centennial Trail parallels the road here.) At the top of the hill bear **R** and continue to Cedar Hill Road.

(14) (16.0 km) Turn **R** onto Cedar Hill Road. A further 300 metres you'll turn **L** onto Feltham Road. Follow Feltham across Shelbourne Street and pass the Lambrick Park/Gordon Head Recreation Centre on the **L**.

(15) (18.2 km) Turn **R** onto Gordon Head Road and then **L** at the light-controlled intersection 300 metres away onto Edgelow Street.

(16) (19.3 km) Turn **R** onto Finnerty Road and continue through the traffic lights to University Drive. Turn **R** here. Leave the drive by turning **R** at the City Centre sign.

(17) (21.1 km) Turn **L** at the traffic light onto Cedar Hill Cross Road and ride the short distance back to Henderson Recreation Centre's carpark on your **R**.

Glencoe Cove/Kwatsech Park

CORDOVA BAY / ISLAND VIEW BEACH / CENTRAL SAANICH

Although this ride has its start and finish in a suburban setting, the majority of the route takes you past the farms, fields and shores that lie to the east of the Pat Bay Highway in Central Saanich.

The shores you'll see are of Cordova Bay opposite the ride's start at the Cordova Bay Plaza (the beach-side Agate Park can be accessed across the road from the plaza at the end of Agate Lane), while the waters at Island View Beach Regional Park lie about 10 kilometres into the ride. Both offer quiet areas to picnic or to just pause and absorb the views. Both shorelines look out over Haro Strait to the San Juan Islands and the Cascade Mountains beyond. (Look for the white dome of Mt. Baker on clear days.)

Hunt and Welch Roads are thoroughly rural and you'll come across livestock, horse paddocks, produce stands and, as Welch turns onto

Martindale Road, a kiwi farm.

I've devised this route as an attractive alternative to the Lochside Trail (even though the ride uses part of the trail), and, apart from one hill, it is basically a flat route.

General description   A ride through the open farmlands of Saanich and eastern Central Saanich with an excursion to the seashore at Island View Beach.

Location   Saanich and Central Saanich about 15 kilometres from Victoria.

Length   32 kilometres. (Two short-cuts offer 27 and 22 kilometre rides.)

Level   Easy.

Start   Cordova Bay Plaza parking area.

Highlights   Some of the Saanich Peninsula's finest farmland; visit to Island View Beach Regional Park; roadside produce stands and barns; start and finish in the oceanside suburb of Cordova Bay.

How to get there   From

downtown take Blanshard Street (which becomes Pat Bay Highway). At about eight kilometres take the Royal Oak Drive exit. Turn **R** onto Royal Oak Drive and after about three kilometres take a **L** onto Cordova Bay Road at a traffic-lighted 4-way intersection. Cordova Bay Plaza is roughly four kilometres along Cordova Bay Road on your **L**. There is ample parking at the shopping centre.

THE RIDE

① From the Plaza's parking area turn **L** onto Cordova Bay Road. You'll pass Mattick's Farm Market on your **R** after 1 kilometre.

② (1.4 km) Turn **R** onto Lochside Drive. After you ride past Lochside Park **R**, the road becomes the gravel surface of Lochside Trail.

③ (2.3 km) At the first crossing turn **R** onto Hunt Road. Pass Dooley Road at 4 km. Hunt becomes Welch Road at a sharp **R** bend.

④ (5.2 km) Turn **L** onto Martindale Road. A local landmark, the kiwi farm, is on your **L** at this intersection. It is surrounded by a stand of tall poplar trees.

⑤ (6.6 km) Turn **R** onto Lochside Drive. (The Pat Bay Highway is 250 metres further on.)

⑥ (7.9 km) Turn **R** onto Island View Road (A large farmer's market barn is on the **L** at this intersection.) (* See p.74 for an alternative route.)

⑦ (10.6 km) Following a steep uphill and "S" bend downhill is the carpark for Island View Beach Regional Park.

⑧ (13.4 km) After returning along Island View Road from the park, turn **R** back onto Lochside Drive. At the entrance to Saanich Historical Artifacts Society's Heritage Acres bear **L** onto the gravel Lochside Trail.

⑨ (16.1 km) Turn **R** onto Mount Newton Cross Road. After 100 metres turn **L** at the stop sign onto the continuation of Lochside Drive. (** See p.74 for alternative route.)

⑩ (18.9 km) Turn **L** onto Amity Drive. Take the pedestrian overpass immediately on your **R** over the Pat Bay Highway. Off the overpass continue up Amity for about 100 metres to take Bourne Terrace on your **L**. Bourne soon becomes Central Saanich Road.

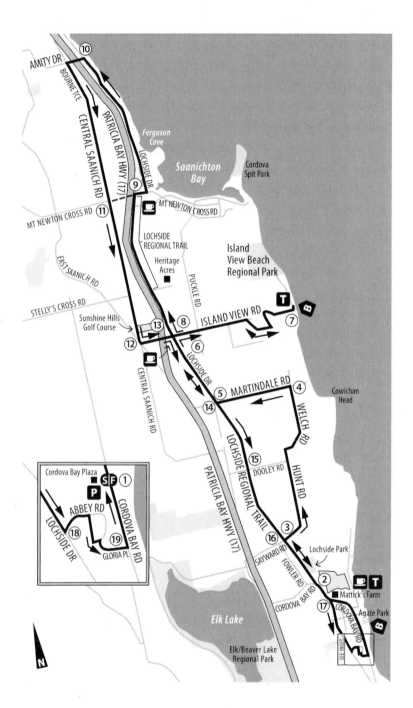

⑪	(21.7 km)	Cross Mount Newton Cross Road.
⑫	(24.0 km)	Turn **L** onto East Saanich Road and then **L** at the well-signed access to the Pat Bay Highway onto Island View Road. Cross the highway at the lights.
⑬	(24.5 km)	Turn **R** onto Lochside Drive at the barn.
⑭	(26.2 km)	Cross Martindale Road.
⑮	(27.5 km)	Cross Dooley Road onto the gravelled Lochside Trail.
⑯	(28.9 km)	Cross Hunt Road.
⑰	(29.7 km)	After passing Lochside Park **L** take the paved trail to your **L** just before Lochside Drive meets Cordova Bay Road. Ride to the lights at Mattick's Farm. Cross to the west side of Cordova Bay Road and turn **L** to take the paved trail that runs parallel to the road. Keep **R** as the trail joins Lochside Drive. Continue on Lochside.
⑱	(31.2 km)	Turn sharp **L** down Abbey Road. This twists and turns down the hill. Keep to your **R** and then take Gloria Place on your **R**.
⑲	(31.7 km)	Turn **L** onto Cordova Bay Road. Ride the 400 metres back to the shopping centre carpark.

* You can save yourself 5 km by continuing on Lochside.

** To save another 5 km you can cross the Pat Bay Highway over the pedestrian overpass to ride the short distance on Mount Newton Cross Road to Central Saanich Road. Turn **L** onto this road and bike to ⑫.

"I told you it was my turn next!"

PANORAMA RECREATION CENTRE / ARDMORE DRIVE

This ride will take you from one side of the Saanich Peninsula to the other and in so doing straddles the municipalities of Central and North Saanich from east to west and back again.

You begin by riding along the farming bench lands that overlook the Pat Bay Highway and Haro Strait. You're able to see James Island and behind that Sidney Island with its finger-shaped spit at its north end. To the south of Sidney Island is the infamous D'Arcy Island which, between 1891 and 1924, was a leper colony for Chinese immigrant workers. It has been a marine park since 1961 and is now part of the Gulf Island National Park Reserve established in May of 2003. If the skies are clear you'll also be able to see the towering dome of the volcanic Mount Baker.

There are two smallish communities that you'll ride through. The first is Saanichton at the intersection of East Saanich Road and Wallace Drive. The other is Brentwood Bay where Wallace meets West Saanich Road. Both have a decent collection of stores, cafés and a pub each. Saanichton also has a museum.

The second half of the ride takes you along the west shores of the peninsula. Its not until you're on Ardmore Drive however, that you get the opportunity to see the Saanich Inlet. There's a beach access at the end of Braemar Avenue that bisects Ardmore and then there's Coles Bay Regional Park off Inverness Road. Both offer good views of the water, the latter opening onto the sheltered Coles Bay.

General description   This loop route crisscrosses the Saanich Peninsula and passes through the two small communities of Brentwood Bay and Saanichton.

Location   Central and North Saanich.

Length   25 kilometres.

Level   Easy.

Start   Panorama Recreation Centre carpark off East Saanich Road.

Highlights   Views east to the islands in Haro Strait; beach access off Ardmore Drive onto the Saanich Inlet; two pubs in the two small communities.

How to get there   Take Blanshard Street/Pat Bay Highway (#17) out of town. After about 25 kilometres turn **L** onto McTavish Road (Airport turnoff). Another .5 kilometres turn **L** onto East Saanich Road. The entrance to the Panorama Recreation Centre carpark is four hundred metres on the **R** off Forest Park Road.

THE RIDE

①   From the recreation centre's carpark turn **R** down Forest Park Road then turn **R** onto East Saanich Road.

② (0.9 km)   Turn **L** onto Lowe Road immediately past Environment Canada's Centre for Plant Health. This road turns **R** to become Emard Terrace and then, as the road bears **L**, it becomes Moxon Terrace. Moxon soon becomes Amity Drive. (This sounds complicated but it's not. There's a single yellow line that follows the contours of the eastward slope.)

③ (1.7 km)   Turn **L** off Amity onto Aldous Terrace. Aldous becomes Wallace Drive at the border between North and Central Saanich.

④ (4.0 km)   At the stop sign turn **L** onto East Saanich Road (Saanich Pioneer Museum is directly opposite) then **R** at the following 4-way stop onto the continuation of Wallace Drive. Cross Mt. Newton Cross Road and, after a further kilometre you'll pass Centennial Park on your **R**.

⑤ (7.7 km)   With the Blue Coyote pub on your **R** and Trafalgar Square shopping centre on your **L** you're now in Brentwood Bay. Turn **R** here onto West Saanich Road.

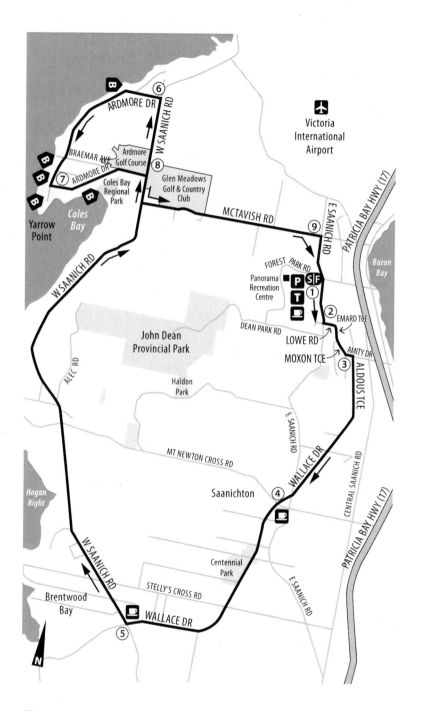

Victoria
International
Airport

ARDMORE DR

W SAANICH RD

6

B

BRAEMAR AVE

Ardmore
Golf Course

7

ARDMORE DR

8

Glen Meadows
Golf & Country
Club

Coles Bay
Regional
Park

B

B

B

B

Yarrow
Point

Coles
Bay

W SAANICH RD

MCTAVISH RD

E SAANICH RD

PATRICIA BAY HWY (17)

Bazan
Bay

9

FOREST PARK RD

Panorama
Recreation
Centre

P

T

S F

1

2

EMARD TCE

DEAN PARK RD

LOWE RD

MOXON TCE

3

AMITY DR

ALDOUS TCE

John Dean
Provincial Park

ALEC RD

Haldon
Park

E SAANICH RD

MT NEWTON CROSS RD

WALLACE DR

Saanichton

4

CENTRAL SAANICH RD

PATRICIA BAY HWY (17)

Hagan
Bight

W SAANICH RD

Centennial
Park

STELLY'S CROSS RD

E SAANICH RD

Brentwood
Bay

WALLACE DR

5

N

⑥ (16.8 km) Just before a sharp **R** bend, turn **L** onto Ardmore Drive. (You've seen this name before a couple of kilometres back on your **L**.)

⑦ (19.4 km) An abrupt turn brings Ardmore back, crescent-like, to West Saanich Road.

⑧ (20.9 km) Turn **R** onto West Saanich Road and then, after 400 metres turn **L** onto McTavish Road.

⑨ (24.2 km) At the 4-way stop turn **R** onto East Saanich Road riding the .8 km back to Forest Park Drive and the recreation centre's carpark.

View of Gulf Islands from Central Saanich Road.

BAZAN BAY / CENTRAL SAANICH

Shaped like a thin rectangle, this route takes you into the farmlands of the eastern part of Central and North Saanich. The roads are straight and for the most part flat — perfect for a not-too-strenuous afternoon ride.

The ride's start is at Cy Hampson Park on the shores of Bazan Bay. Originally known as Bazan Bay Park it was renamed in 1997 for Cy Hampson, a longtime resident of the area and a keen conservationist and biologist. At the turn-around point at the end of Central Saanich Road is the Silver Rill Farm — well known for its late-summer corn and other farm produce.

As you pass through the community of Saanichton you have access to a pub, cafés and stores plus a local museum and forestry centre. On your way back along East Saanich Road you'll see the treed slopes of John Dean Park's Mount Newton.

Access to the park is via the steep 2.5 kilometre Dean Park Road. Just past the park access is the Canadian government's Centre for Plant Health on the right with the small Dominion Brook Park adjacent to it.

General description A rectangular loop through farmlands and the small community of Saanichton.

Location The eastern side of Central and North Saanich.

Length 15 kilometres.

Level Easy.

Start Cy Hampson Park (Bazan Bay).

Highlights Rural roads; Saanichton village and its amenities; roadside produce stands.

How to get there Take Blanshard Street /Pat Bay Highway (#17) out of town. After 22 kilometres turn **R** onto Amity. (This is not a major intersection and is just before a pedestrian overpass.) Turn quickly **L** onto Lochside Drive. After a kilometre turn **R** into Cy Hampson Park's carpark.

Overpass at McTavish Exchange.

THE RIDE

① From the park's carpark turn **L** onto Lochside Drive and ride the kilometre to Amity Drive.

② (1.0 km) Turn **R** onto Amity and cross the highway via the footbridge.

③ (1.1 km) After 100 metres turn **L** onto Bourne Road (which soon becomes Central Saanich Road).

④ (3.5 km) Cross Mt. Newton Cross Road. For a shorter ride, i.e. 10 km, turn **R** here and ride up to East Saanich Road and the village of Saanichton turning **R** onto East Saanich Road. (Go to ⑥ for short cut.)

⑤ (6.0 km) Turn sharp **R** onto East Saanich Road. (Shady Creek Church is 400 metres on the **L**.)

⑥ (8.7 km) Cross Mt. Newton Cross Road — again. You're now in the village of Saanichton. The Prairie Inn Pub is at this intersection on the **L**. Continue through the next stop sign keeping to East Saanich Road. You soon pass the Saanich Pioneer Museum **L** and the Saanich Forestry Centre **R**.

⑦ (11.6 km) Dean Park Road is on the **L** which leads to the entrance of John Dean Provincial Park. A picnic area is on the **R**.

⑧ (13.1 km) Having past the Panorama Recreation Centre on your **L** turn **R** onto McTavish Road.

⑨ (13.7 km) Cross the Pat Bay Highway via the overpass of the McTavish Interchange and turn **R** onto Lochside Drive.

⑩ (15.0 km) Turn **L** into the Cy Hampson Park carpark.

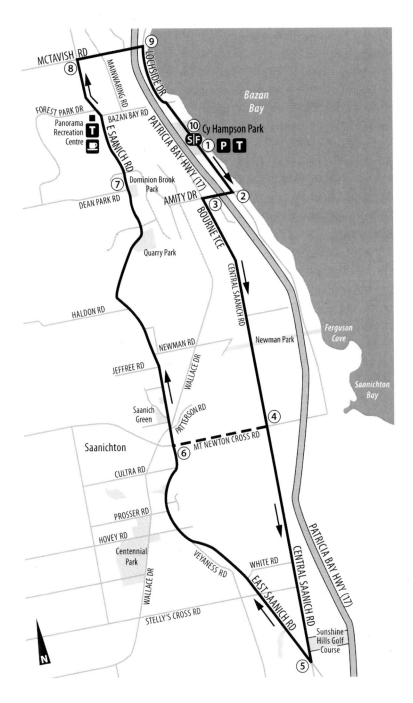

MCTAVISH RD

⑨

⑧

MAINWARING RD

LOCHSIDE DR

PATRICIA BAY HWY (17)

Bazan Bay

FOREST PARK DR

Panorama Recreation Centre

BAZAN BAY RD

E SAANICH RD

⑩ Cy Hampson Park

S F ① P T

Dominion Brook Park

⑦

DEAN PARK RD

AMITY DR

③

②

BOURNE TCE

Quarry Park

CENTRAL SAANICH RD

HALDON RD

NEWMAN RD

Newman Park

JEFFREE RD

WALLACE DR

Ferguson Cove

Saanich Green

PATTERSON RD

Saanichton Bay

④

Saanichton

⑥ MT NEWTON CROSS RD

CULTRA RD

PROSSER RD

HOVEY RD

Centennial Park

WALLACE DR

VEYANESS RD

WHITE RD

EAST SAANICH RD

CENTRAL SAANICH RD

PATRICIA BAY HWY (17)

STELLY'S CROSS RD

Sunshine Hills Golf Course

⑤

N

BAZAN BAY / DEEP COVE / CURTEIS POINT / SIDNEY

The northern tip of the Saanich Peninsula is great for the cyclist. The roads are safe with good surfaces, few intersections and little traffic. Despite one or two short and steep hills, the terrain is mostly undulating and, apart from the first few kilometres of this route, you're riding pretty close to open water.

The major commercial landmarks of the area are two transportation terminals — the Victoria International Airport and the BC Ferries Terminal. You'll ride by both of these. But the area is interesting for its other well-known features. There is Patricia Bay with its seaplane base and small park. In Deep Cove, along Chalet Road, you find the Chalet Restaurant and Vineyard, the former well-established and high-end. The aptly named Lands End Road follows the very tip of the peninsula and, between the

houses, gives grand views over Satellite Channel and Colburne Passage to Mt. Tuam on Salt Spring Island.

As you pass the ferry terminal the route takes you into Curteis Point — a delightful and scenic protrusion off the main peninsula. The point is a perfect example of the numerous enclaves in the Greater Victoria area that give you a sense of tranquility and of being "far from the madding crowd." On the ride back you ride pass marinas along the shores of Tsehum Harbour and through the town of Sidney. In Sidney you'll find a variety of stores, restaurants and cafés and, probably the largest number of bookstores per capita anywhere in the country.

General description   A large loop route around the tip of the Saanich Pensinsula. Because you're on coastal roads for the

Deep Cove.

main part there are few intersections which makes for a scenically pleasing and safe ride.

Location In the municipality of North Saanich and the town of Sidney.

Length 32 kilometres.

Level Easy to moderate.

Start Cy Hampson Park carpark on the shores of Bazan Bay in North Saanich.

Highlights Patricia Bay Park; Chalet and Lands End Roads; Curteis Point; the town of Sidney; Bazan Bay.

How to get there Take Blanshard Street/Pat Bay Highway (#17) out of town. After about 22 kilometres turn **R** onto Amity Drive and then **L** onto Lochside Drive. Cy Hampson Park is 400 metres on your **R**.

THE RIDE

①		Exit the park's carpark and turn **R** onto Lochside Drive.
②	(1.1 km)	Turn **L** onto the McTavish Interchange using the overpass. Take the McTavish exit Road onto McTavish Road.
③	(1.9 km)	Turn **R** onto East Saanich Road at the 4-way stop.
④	(2.4 km)	Turn **L** onto Willingdon Road at the roundabout.

⑤	(3.3 km)	Turn **L** onto Willingdon again at the entrance to the airport.
⑥	(5.3 km)	Turn **R** onto West Saanich Road. The seaplane base is across the road as is Patricia Bay Park.
⑦	(8.3 km)	Having left the shores of Patricia Bay you now turn **L** onto Downey Road.
⑧	(10.0 km)	At the end of a steep descent turn **R** onto Madrona Drive. You now follow the road around Coal Point and onto Deep Cove. As an uphill begins you'll pass the Deep Cove Marina on your **L**.
⑨	(11.8 km)	As Madrona becomes Birch Road turn **L** onto Chalet Road. Two kilometres along Chalet you'll pass the Chalet Estate Winery on your **R** and on your **L** the Deep Cove Chalet Restaurant. After a further two kilometres Chalet becomes Lands End Road and continues as such until you meet the Pat Bay Highway.
⑩	(20.0 km)	Cross the highway and continue across the next traffic light for a further 200 metres.
⑪		Turn **L** onto Curteis Road. You'll now enter Curteis Point — a rather hilly two-kilometre circuit. Curteis soon becomes Dunne Road which, as you turn **L** becomes Kedge Anchor Road. This road in turn becomes Inwood Road. Follow Inwood until it intersects Tryon Road.
⑫		Turn **R** on Tryon.
⑬	(22.8 km)	At the end of Tryon turn **L** along a narrow road signed Lochside Trail. This will take you to a path that parallels the highway.
⑭		After passing beside a footbridge turn **L** along McDonald Park Road. Cross McDonald and continue on the marked bike lane on McDonald toward Sidney.
⑮	(25.4 km)	Just past the North Saanich School turn **L** onto Resthaven Drive.
⑯	(28.1 km)	You're now in downtown Sidney. Turn **L** at the traffic lights onto Beacon Avenue and then first **R** at the next lights onto Fifth Street. This street becomes Lochside Drive which you'll take for about four kilometres until turning **L** into Cy Hampson Park.

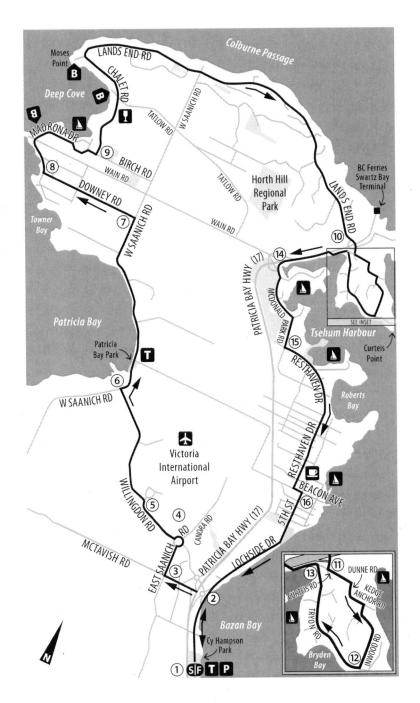

AIRPORT / GLAMORGAN ROAD

The idea of circling an airport on a bike might not be terribly appealing, that is, if you concentrate only on dead flat runways, terminal buildings and chain-link fences. This particular ride however, although circling the Victoria International Airport, takes you past two delightful locations. The first is Holy Trinity Church at the corner of Mills Road and West Saanich Road. Its original wooden church and well-kempt yard were first established in 1885 and are now designated as a BC heritage site.

Less than a couple of kilometres away is another historical site — that of Glamorgan Farm. Richard John, a Welshman who named the place after the county in Wales where he was born, created the farm over two centuries ago in 1805. Originally a 202-hectare property, it has, over time, been whittled down to just 3.4 hectares.

Nevertheless, the original farm buildings, many of which are of log construction, are still standing. Though considerably smaller than in its glory days, the farm is still a major contributor to maintaining the rural nature of the northern end of the Saanich Peninsula.

General description
A short, flat loop that passes two historical sites while circling the Victoria International Airport.

Location   The municipality of North Saanich.

Length   11 kilometres.

Level   Easy.

Start   Rideau Avenue **R** off Canora Road just past the McTavish Interchange.

Highlights   Holy Trinity Church and churchyard; the two-century old Glamorgan Farm; two possible lunch stops: a café and a pub; BC Aviation Museum.

How to get there   Take Blanshard Street/Pat Bay Highway (#17) out of town.

Relaxing at Patricia Bay Park.

After 23 kilometres follow the Airport signage on the McTavish Interchange. As you turn **R** onto Canora Road after the second roundabout, Rideau Avenue is on the **R**.

THE RIDE

①   From Rideau Avenue turn **R** onto Canora Road. After 200 metres bear **L** onto Willingdon Road. (A roundabout soon follows.)

② (1.5 km)   At the Airport Terminal entrance continue straight on Willingdon.

③ (3.5 km)   Turn **R** onto West Saanich Road. (A seaplace base and Patricia Bay Park are across the road.)

④ (4.4 km)   Turn **R** onto Mills Road. (The old Holy Trinity Church is on this corner.)

⑤ (5.2 km)   Turn **L** onto Littlewood Road (Just past the municipal hall.)

⑥ (5.6 km)   Bear **R** onto Glamorgan Road. Shortly, on your **R**, is the historic Glamorgan Farm and the community allotment gardens.

⑦ (6.7 km)   Turn **R** onto McDonald Park Road. Half a kilometre further you cross Mills Road at the stop sign. At a short **L** bend McDonald Park Road becomes Beacon Avenue.

⑧ (8.2 km)   Turn **R** onto Stirling Way before Beacon Avenue intersects the Pat Bay Highway. This road curves in front of the main airport runway after which it becomes Ocean Avenue.

⑨ (9.7 km)   Turn **L** onto Canora Road. (On the **L** is Mary's Blue Moon Café and further on, on the **R** is the BC Aviation Museum.) Keep to Canora at the next intersection.

⑩ (11.0 km)   Bear **L** as Canora goes to meet the interchange and then turn **L** onto Rideau Avenue.

(A paved, multi-use trail now circles the airport and can be easily accessed.)

WAIN ROAD / DEEP COVE

This brief foray into the rural northern part of the Saanich Peninsula will not disappoint riders with an inclination towards either garden nurseries or horses or both. The two long roads you'll ride offer both of the above. Wain Road is noted for its two large nurseries both of which are on the right-hand side as you ride west. Tatlow Road has a number of stables on either side of the road plus good views of open pastureland. However, no matter what your inclinations are (apart from having a good bike ride) this ride offers a glimpse into a very picturesque part of the peninsula.

You can also take advantage

Winery and restaurant in Deep Cove.

of a short walk down to Chalet Beach on the shores of Deep Cove (at Tatlow Road's west end) or explore some of the trails of Horth Hill Regional Park (at Tatlow's east end).

Both of these potential excursions offer great views — Chalet Beach, across Saanich Inlet; Horth Hill Park, of the peninsula, Salt Spring Island and the surrounding islands.

General description   A short flat loop route that goes into the rural centre of North Saanich.

Location   The municipality of North Saanich 28 kilometres north of Victoria.

Length   10 kilometres.

Level   Easy.

Start   Blue Heron Park's parking area off McDonald Park Road.

Highlights   Quiet rural roads with light traffic; possible picnic on Chalet Beach; lots of horses; two large nurseries.

How to get there   Take Blanshard Street/Pat Bay Highway out of town. At 28 kilometres and a kilometre past the main entrance into Sidney's downtown — Beacon Avenue — turn **R** onto McDonald Park Road (immediately past the pedestrian overpass). Continue on McDonald Park Road for another kilometre to take a **L** turn into the Blue Heron Park (just past Parkland School). Once in the park turn **L** into the first carpark.

THE RIDE

① From the park's carpark ride back down to McDonald Park Road and turn **L**.

② (0.5 km) Turn **L** onto the Pat Bay Highway overpass. (Follow directions to Wain Road)

③ (1.0 km) Turn **L** onto Wain Road at the intersection.

④ (3.1 km) Turn **R** onto West Saanich Road (A firehall is across the road.)

⑤ (3.3 km) Turn **L** onto Birch Road (There is a store and a gas station here.)

⑥ (4.4 km) Turn **R** onto Chalet Road.

⑦ (5.4 km) Turn **R** onto Tatlow Road (The Chalet Estate Winery and the Chalet Restaurant are located at this junction. Turning **L** here will take you to Chalet Beach at the end of Tatlow.) After a further kilometre cross West Saanich Road.

⑧   (8.1 km)   The entrance to Horth Hill Park on **L**.

⑨   (8.7 km)   Turn **L** back onto Wain Road.

⑩   (9.3 km)   Turn **R** onto the overpass. (Follow directions to McDonald Park Road.)

⑪   (9.8 km)   Turn **R** onto McDonald Park Road.

⑫   (10.0 km)   Turn **R** into Blue Heron Park riding back to your car.

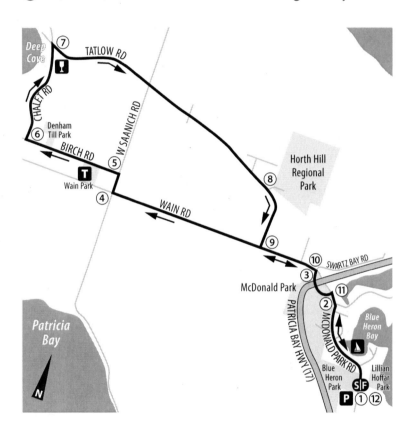

BLUE HERON PARK / LANDS END ROAD

One would imagine that the planning department of North Saanich municipality had little difficulty deciding the name for the road that traverses the end of the Saanich Peninsula. It is indeed land's end. With the water of Tsehum Harbour, Canoe Bay and Swartz Bay forming its north-eastern shores; Colburne Passage and Satellite Channel its northern shore and Deep Cove and the much larger Saanich Inlet its north-western shore, the road spans a spectacular portion of this large peninsula.

One of the things you'll notice as you ride this neck-of-the-woods is the preponderance of trailhead signs. Although hiking trails are not the focus of the ride it will give you some idea of the many trail options in this still heavily forested area.

There are however, a couple of nice beach accesses to pause at if the desire takes you. One

is Moses Point Road. This rocky shore is a beachcomber's paradise, especially at low tide when the tidal pools come alive with tiny crabs, starfish and other miniature seashore life. The other access is at the end of Tatlow Road just before the Chalet Winery and Restaurant. This is called Chalet Beach and is a favoured spot for high summer swimming.

On your way back you'll ride along the cycling-friendly Wain Road. Straight as a die and not too hilly, the road is named after Henry Wain, an enterprising pioneer of the area who, besides being a carpenter and hop grower, served as the local mail-carrier transporting mail to and from Victoria in his stagecoach.

General description   A mildly undulating ride through the northern section of Saanich Peninsula. Characterized by spectacular views of water and surrounding islands, heavily forested uplands and large waterfront homes and landscaped gardens, it will be hard not to linger and explore.

Location   The northern tip of Saanich Peninsula.

Length   16 kilometres.

Level   Moderate.

Start   The Blue Heron Park car-park off McDonald Road north of Sidney.

Highlights   Great views of Salt Spring Island; Colburne Passage and Satellite Channel; beach accesses to explore; only one steep but short hill; voyeuristic opportunities to goggle at large waterfront mansions.

How to get there   Take Blanshard Street/Pat Bay Highway (#17) out of town. About 28 kilometres out of town and a kilometre past Sidney's Beacon Avenue, turn **R** onto

McDonald Park Road. Continue on McDonald for another kilometre and turn **L** into Blue Heron Park — just past Parkland School. Park in the first available parking area.

Curteis Point.

THE RIDE

① From the park's carpark area turn **L** onto McDonald Park Road.

② (0.5 km) Bear **L** taking the Lochside Trail that parallels the highway. (You'll brush pass the ramp to a pedestrian overpass.)

③ (1.7 km) At a stop sign cross onto Curteis Road. After about 200 metres turn **L** onto Lands End Road. You'll soon cross the highway. Keep to Lands End Road for the next eight kilometres.

④ (6.0 km) West Saanich Road is on the **L**. (This is a possible short-cut and saves about 5 km. If you take it turn **L** at ⑨ below onto Wain Road.)

⑤	(8.3 km)	Moses Point beach access on **R**.
⑥	(9.1 km)	Tatlow Road beach access **R**. Chalet Estate Winery **L** and the Chalet Restaurant **R**.
⑦	(10.1 km)	Turn **R** onto Birch Road. (A steep downhill follows after 300 metres.) Birch becomes Madrona Drive.
⑧	(11.5 km)	Turn **L** onto Wain Road at a wide **L** bend. Coal Point Lane is opposite.
⑨	(13.5 km)	Cross West Saanich Road (firehall is on **L**.)
⑩	(14.7 km)	Tatlow Road/Horth Hill Park entrance on **L**.
⑪	(15.2 km)	Turn **R** following the McDonald Park signs onto the highway overpass.
⑫	(15.7 km)	Turn **R** onto McDonald Park Road riding the short distance back to Blue Heron Park.

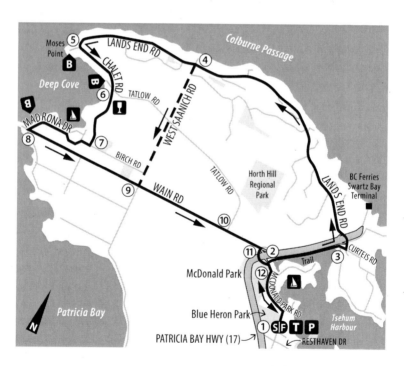

TOUR OF THE HIGHLANDS

Although this ride starts and finishes on the southern edge of the Saanich Peninsula, the majority of the time you'll be riding through the rural municipality of Highlands. Aptly named, this is one of the most hilly yet scenically pleasing areas of Greater Victoria. Yes, there are patches of farmland but, for the most part, the land is wooded. The reason for this is twofold: first, its residents prefer to keep the forest intact for ecological, aesthetic and privacy reasons. Second, as you might appreciate once you've ridden the route, a large part of the municipality has been, over the years, appropriated as parkland, both by the provincial government and by the Capital Regional District. The largest of the parks is the Gowlland-Tod Provincial Park. Established in 1995, the park comprises well over 1200 hectares and has

two distinct habitats. One is the forested upland hills and bluffs and the other coastal — along the waters of Saanich Inlet and Finlayson Arm. The smallest park is the regional Lone Tree Hill Park, once noticeable for, you've guessed it, the singular, stunted conifer perched at the park's apex. Two other regional parks — Mt. Work and Francis/King, lie within the municipality and are both spectacular in different ways. Francis/King for its deep coniferous forest and Mt. Work for its splendid views from the area's highest point of 450 metres. All four parks are easily accessible from the route of your ride — if you have the time, inclination or energy to explore them.

General description
A hilly ride into the heart of the Highlands. Passes or goes through four of the region's most spectacular parks.

Location   Starts and finishes in Saanich about 10 kilometres north of downtown Victoria.

Length   36 kilometres.

Level   Moderate to strenuous.

Start   Carpark adjacent to two stores on West Saanich Road.

Highlights   Little traffic, narrow; hilly roads and deep forested areas.

How to get there   Take Blanshard Street to the outskirts of the city where it becomes the Pat Bay Highway (#17). After about 8 kilometres take the Royal Oak Drive exit and turn **L**. Continue over the highway turning **R** at the third traffic light onto West Saanich Road. Park in the carpark of two stores 400 metres on the **R**.

THE RIDE

①		From the carpark turn **R** onto West Saanich Road. Pass the entrance to the Centre of the Universe after three kilometres on the **R**. (It's a 1.5 km hill climb to the observatory.)
②	(5.5 km)	Turn **L** onto Wallace Drive just past the Red Barn Market on the **L**.
③	(6.0 km)	Turn **L** again onto Willis Point Road.
④	(10.0 km)	It's now **L** on Ross-Durrance Road — a winding, hilly road that takes you into the heart of the rugged Highlands municipality. Immediately you pass the entrances to both Mount Work Regional Park **R** and Gowlland-Tod Provincial Park **L**. (Note: Ross-Durrance becomes Millstream Lake Road so don't be confused at your next intersection.)
⑤	(16.3 km)	At the stop sign turn sharply **L** onto Munn Road. This road skirts Mount Work's southern entrance before bisecting Francis/King Regional Park just before its intersection with Prospect Lake Road.
⑥	(25.6 km)	Turn **L** onto Prospect Lake Road. At 30 km Prospect Lake comes into view on the **R**. A further 1.5 km is the small Whitehead Park with beach access and picnic area.
⑦	(32.0 km)	Turn **R** onto West Saanich Road. Across the road are a grocery store, gas station and a restaurant.
⑧	(36.0 km)	Turn **L** into the carpark where the ride began.

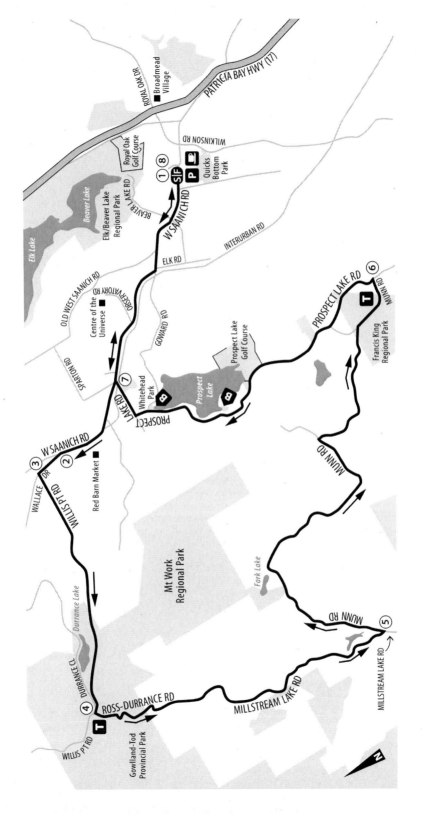

TOUR OF SAANICH

Among local riding enthusiasts this ride is perhaps the most popular and, more than any other, defines riding enjoyment in the Victoria area.

Though not a terribly hilly route, the ride takes you closest to local waters for the longest possible time as you will ever get.

Looking at the ride's map you'll note right away that you're effectively riding around the perimeter of a large peninsula. On its eastern side you're overlooking Haro Strait, a wide body of water that separates, at this point, the southeastern part of Vancouver Island and the San Juan Islands of the United States. On clear days you can see the volcanic peak of Mt. Baker rising above the not too far off islands of San Juan and Orcas.

The waters of the western shore are of the Saanich Inlet — a deep and incisive stretch of water that divides the peninsula from the main island. As you ride this coastline you get views of the wooded slopes of the Malahat summit and, to the north, the community of Mill Bay. You'll also ride into the charming enclave of Deep Cove. Its classy restaurant with a winery across the road; its twisty shore-hugging lanes and selection of attractive waterfront homes make it one of the highlights of this spectacular ride.

The north end of the peninsula is traversed by the undulations of Lands End Road. Besides getting great views of Salt Spring Island across Satellite Channel you'll ride past some of the most expensive real estate in Canada. In 2006, one home on Lands End Road was on offer for 18 million dollars. You'll judge for yourself whether it would be worth that much to live in that neck of the woods.

Once past the community of Brentwood Bay, you lose

Tandems --— out in the country.

*the water but what you gain
are rolling pastures and thick
roadside forest. Although the city
is only a few kilometres away,
you'd never know it riding the
route back to Broadmead.*

General description As one
of the longer rides in the book,
you'll get a good taste of what
Greater Victoria has on offer.
Don't be put off by the distance,
there are few steep hills on this
circular route which can be
accomplished by a good novice
rider who likes a challenge. There
is the possibility of overnight stays
in Sidney and Brentwood Bay or
you can divide the route into two
of three sections to be completed
over a few weeks. There are long
flat sections especially along the
Lochside Trail.

Location Saanich, Central
Saanich, North Saanich.

Length 66 or 93 kilometres.

Level Moderate.

Start Broadmead Village
Shopping Centre's carpark.

Highlights Coastline views —
east and west; rural roads; town
of Sidney; Lands End Road and
views of Salt Spring Island; Deep
Cove; Brentwood Bay.

How to get there   Take Blanshard Street out of town. Continue on Pat Bay Highway (#17) and, after eight kilometres, take the Royal Oak Drive exit turning **R** onto Royal Oak Drive. The entrance to Broadmead Village Shopping Centre carpark is 100 metres on the **R**.

THE RIDE

① Exit the Broadmead Village Shopping Centre parking lot and turn **R** onto Royal Oak Drive.

② (2.03 km) Turn **L** at the four-way traffic lights onto Cordova Bay Road. You'll pass Mattick's Farm at 6 km. Cordova Bay Road becomes Fowler Road shortly after.

③ (7.2 km) Turn **R** onto Hunt Road. (Sayward Road hill goes to the **L**.) Hunt becomes Welch Road at 8.8 km.

④ (10.2 km) Turn **L** onto Martindale Road. There's a row of poplar trees on your **L** bordering a kiwi orchard.

⑤ (11.9 km) Turn **R** onto the Pat Bay Highway. (There is a wide shoulder on the highway for the four kilometres you're on it.)

⑥ (15.8 km) Turn **R** onto Mt. Newton Cross Road. (Quality Inn Motel is on the **L**.)

⑦ (16.0 km) Turn **L** at the stop sign onto Lochside Drive.

⑧ (22.4 km) After passing Tulista Park on your **R**, turn **R** onto Ocean Avenue. You'll pass the Anacortes Ferry Terminal **R**. Ocean becomes 1st Street at this point which, in turn, intersects with Beacon Avenue.

⑨ (23.1 km) Turn **L** onto Beacon Avenue then sharp **R** onto 2nd Street. After a further 200 metres turn **L** onto Mt. Baker Avenue then **R** onto 3rd Street. (Sounds complicated but it's not.)

⑩ (24.3 km) Turn **L** onto Malaview Avenue at the BC Ferries sign.

⑪ (24.7 km) Turn **R** onto Resthaven Drive at the grocery store **R**.

⑫ (26.5 km) Turn **R** onto McDonald Road at the North Saanich School **R**.

⑬ (28.0 km) Turn **R** onto the Pat Bay Highway. Keep to the shoulder and follow signs for Lands End Road.

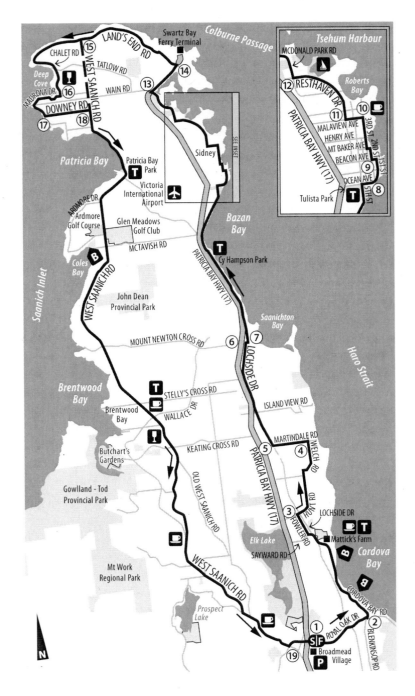

(14) (29.2 km)   Once on the off-ramp move to the **L** and turn **L** at the traffic lights riding over the highway to go straight onto Lands End Road.

(15) (33.4 km)   West Saanich Road to your **L**. (This is a possible alternative route saving about 7 km. You'd join the described route at (18).) At 35.1 km Lands End becomes Chalet Road. At Tatlow Road you'll pass the Chalet Restaurant **R** and the Chalet Estate Winery **L**.

(16) (37.4 km)   Turn **R** onto Birch Road. Birch soon becomes Madrona Drive. Continue on Madrona past Wain Road.

(17) (39.1 km)   Just before Madrona dead ends turn **L** onto Downey Road.

(18) (40.6 km)   Turn **R** onto West Saanich Road. You'll stay on this road for the next 24 kilometres so relax and enjoy the scenery.

(19) (64.8 km)   At the top of a steepish hill is the traffic-light junction of West Saanich Road with Wilkinson Road and Royal Oak Drive. Turn **L** here onto Royal Oak Drive. You soon cross the Pat Bay Highway after which you turn **R** into Broadmead Village Shopping Centre parking lot.

(To create a longer ride of 93 kilometres start by using ride #6 following Cook Street and then taking Maplewood/Blenkinsop Roads out to Royal Oak Drive. Instead of turning **L** at Royal Oak Drive continue straight onto Cordova Bay Road, following the description from there as outlined from (2) on the route above. To return, ride past Broadmead Village Shopping Centre to the intersection of Royal Oak Drive, Cordova Bay Road and Blenkinsop, turning **R** on Blenkinsop then riding back, via Cook Street, to Beacon Hill Park as in ride #6.)

West Shore
(View Royal, Colwood, Langford, Highlands, Metchosin and Sooke)

HIGHLANDS / HUMPBACK ROAD / GALLOPING GOOSE

This nearly 40 kilometre ride is never very far from the country's main vehicular artery — the Trans-Canada Highway. In fact, it starts a stone's throw away from one of its local intersections — the Colwood exit. But don't be discouraged. The route described here draws a large circle around the highway and takes you into the hills on both its flanks. For the most part you'll never know it's there. Like other rides in this book that go into the Highlands and Langford areas this one has its fair share of ups and downs. The one "down" that is spectacular is the descent off Millstream Road along Finlayson

Arm Road and into Goldstream Provincial Park. The west side of Mt. Finlayson rises precipitously above your left shoulder while the marshy waters of the butt-end of Finlayson Arm lay below to your right as you follow the twisting road through the tall conifers on its way to Goldstream Park.

Once across the Trans-Canada you enter the eastern edge of the Sooke Hills. This large forested area has now become a wilderness preserve. Humpback Road squeezes between two of the area's smaller mounts — Mount McDonald and Mount Wells. You see information signs *along the road indicating the hiking trails that ribbon these hills.*

The final stretch of the ride takes you along the Galloping Goose Trail and allows you to relax a little as you trundle along this dead-flat grade.

General description   The route draws a large circle on the western side of Greater Victoria. There are plenty of hills but the major ones are descents. You'll ride through or near four parks and when you're not doing that, it will feel and look like you are.

Location   West of Victoria in the municipalities of Highlands,

Langford, Colwood and View Royal.

Length   38 kilometres.

Level   Moderate to strenuous.

Start   The Galloping Goose Trail's Atkins Road trailhead carpark in View Royal.

Highlights   A ride through one of the region's most hilly and forested areas; great scenery; great exercise.

How to get there   From downtown follow Douglas Street/ Trans-Canada Highway out of town for 10 kilometres. Take the **R** Colwood exit. Almost immediately after the underpass turn **R** into the signed Galloping Goose Trail's, Atkins Road carpark.

THE RIDE

①		From the Galloping Goose Trail's Atkins Road carpark turn **R** onto the trail going east (toward Victoria).
②	(1.1 km)	Turn **L** at a signed 4-way intersection onto Burnside Road West.
③	(2.3 km)	Turn **L** onto Prospect Lake Road.
④	(3.5 km)	Turn **L** onto Munn Road. Half a kilometre on the **R** is the entrance to Francis / King Regional Park. (At 11 km is the trailhead to Mt. Work Regional Park on **R**.)
⑤	(12.9 km)	Turn **L** at the stop sign onto Millstream Lake Road.
⑥	(13.9 km)	At the stop sign turn **L** onto Millstream Road. (Don't be confused.)
⑦	(14.7 km)	Turn **R** onto Finlayson Arm Road. (This road is a mostly narrow and steep downhill.)
⑧	(19.9 km)	You're now at the junction with the Trans-Canada

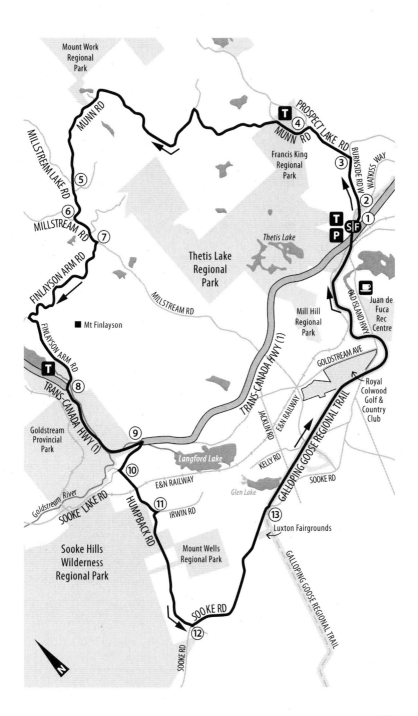

Highway and is also an entrance to Goldstream Provincial Park. (You've just passed the trailhead to the 419 metre Mount Finlayson on your **L**.) Turn **L** onto the highway. (Be careful of the traffic. There is a reasonably wide shoulder and bear in mind you're only on it for 2.5 km.)

⑨ (22.4 km) Turn **R** through the barriers onto Sooke Lake Road.

⑩ (23.2 km) At Ma Miller's Pub turn **L** onto Humpback Road.

⑪ (24.5 km) Take the **R** fork at Humpback and Irwin to continue on Humpback Road. A carpark for Mount Wells Regional Park is just past this fork on the **R**.

⑫ (27.6 km) Turn **L** onto Sooke Road.

⑬ (31.3 km) Just past the Luxton fairground (on your **R**) turn **L** onto Glen Lake Road where you'll see the Galloping Goose Trail on your **R**. Follow the trail back to Atkins Road carpark about seven kilometres away.

Riding past a pub?

ATKINS ROAD / HAPPY VALLEY ROAD / EQUIMALT LAGOON

"West Shore" is a term used for the five municipalities — Colwood, Highlands, Langford, Metchosin and View Royal — that lie to the west of Victoria, and you'll ride through part of four of them.

Although you're never very far from the Galloping Goose Trail, this ride will take you on some of the lesser-known roads of the area. That's not to indicate that you won't encounter a few interesting landmarks. Just the opposite. And perhaps the most impressive is the ride along Ocean Boulevard as it follows the Coburg Peninsula. On the right of the peninsula is Esquimalt Lagoon which provides the foreground for Royal Roads University and its stately Hatley Castle. On the left is the ocean and the view east to Esquimalt's docks, Fisgard Lighthouse and the distant bluffs of Victoria's Beacon Hill Park. As
you ride up from the peninsula you'll pass the historic Fort Rodd Park.

Earlier on in the ride you'll circle Glen Lake and before that you'll pass the entrance to Mill Hill Regional Park. All told, I think you'll find the ride has a nice mix of residential and semi-rural neighbourhoods to explore.

General description This is essentially a loop route with a very short dog-leg finish. There are two major hills — one down and the other up and both come near the end of the ride. Sandwiched in between the two is the scenic Coburg Peninsula.

Location West of Victoria in the municipalities of View Royal, Colwood, Langford and Metchosin.

Length 24 kilometres.

Level Easy to moderate.

Start The Galloping Goose Trail's Atkins Road trailhead carpark in View Royal.

Highlights The ride along the Coburg Peninsula with its views of Royal Roads University, Hatley Castle, Esquimalt Lagoon on one side and the ocean and Victoria's waterfront on the other.

How to get there From downtown follow Douglas Street/ Trans-Canada Highway for 10 kilometres. Take the **R** Colwood exit. Almost immediately after passing under the highway turn **R** into the signed Atkins Road/ Galloping Goose Trail carpark.

THE RIDE

①		From the Galloping Goose Trail's Atkins Road carpark turn **L** (west) onto Atkins Road.
②	(0.5 km)	Cross Six Mile Road.
③	(2.7 km)	Turn **L** at the stop sign to continue on Atkins Avenue. (At 2.9 km is the entrance **R** to Mill Hill Park.)
④	(4.0 km)	Atkins Avenue dead-ends here. Continue by crossing the Veterans Memorial Parkway and turn **L**. Cross Goldstream Avenue and then take Station Avenue which is the first **R** after Goldstream.
⑤	(5.0 km)	Turn **L** onto Jacklin Road.
⑥	(5.5 km)	Turn **R** at the traffic light onto Jenkins Avenue.
⑦	(6.4 km)	Turn **R** at the stop sign onto Glen Lake Road. (Although you're riding close to Glen Lake, unfortunately there are no lake access points along this road.)
⑧	(7.9 km)	Turn **L** onto Sooke Road then immediately **R** onto Happy Valley Road. (Alternatively, you can simply cross Sooke Road and take the Galloping Goose Trail for about a kilometre and join Happy Valley Road at Englewood Avenue.)
⑨	(10.2 km)	Turn **L** onto Latoria Road.
⑩	(14.0 km)	Turn **L** onto Metchosin Road.
⑪	(15.8 km)	Turn **R** onto Lagoon Road at a corner store. (Beware of the steep downhill that follows.)
⑫	(17.0 km)	Turn **L** onto Ocean Boulevard. You are now on the Coburg Peninsula separating Esquimalt Lagoon from open water. Views of Hatley Castle and Royal

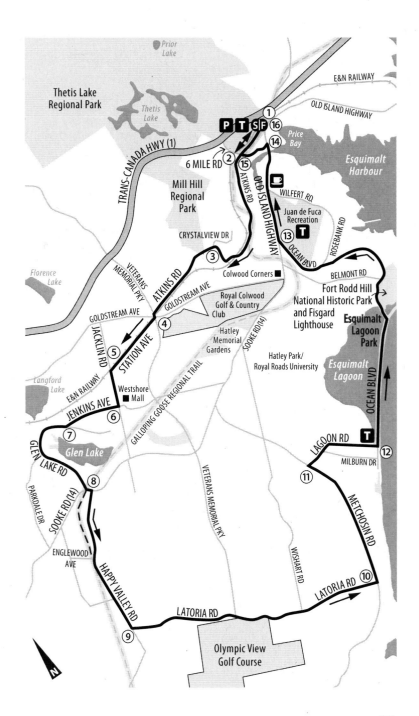

Roads University are on your **L** and of Esquimalt and Victoria on your **R**. About a kilometre after crossing the bridge is the entrance **R** to the Fort Rodd and Fisgard Lighthouse Historical Park.

⑬ (21.3 km) Turn **R** onto the Old Island Highway. (You can access the Galloping Goose Trail here by crossing the highway and following the signs. This will take you back to the start at Atkins Road carpark.)

⑭ (22.8 km) Turn **L** at the traffic light onto Six Mile Road (signed direction Nanaimo).

⑮ (23.8 km) Turn **R** onto Atkins Road.

⑯ (23.8 km) Turn **R** into the Atkins Road Galloping Goose carpark.

View from Esquimalt Lagoon.

TOUR OF METCHOSIN

Although this ride starts and finishes in the municipality of Langford, its major portion goes deep into the sleepy, rural district of Metchosin. The two institutions that Metchosin is noted for are next door to each other (and make unlikely neighbours) — the Lester B. Pearson College of the Pacific and the William Head Prison. Both occupy waterfront property on Pedder Bay and as a result are at the end of dead-end roads. You'll ride within a couple of kilometres of both and while you might not want to visit the prison you might want to tour the beautiful campus of the college.

On the way to the highpoint of the route — up Lindholm and then down Kangaroo you get great views of Pedder Bay, the Strait of Juan de Fuca and the Olympic Mountains. You also pass two popular oceanside regional parks, Devonian and Witty's Lagoon, on your way

back — both worth a visit. The village of Metchosin is rather small as is its church, St. Mary the Virgin. Built in 1885 the church is now a heritage site. If you hit the spring season right you'll find a remarkable display of chocolate lilies in the quaint church's yard.

General description   A circular ride that explores the western half of the rural district of Metchosin. The route takes you down an avenue of century-old Lombardy poplars and passes the entrance of two small waterfront regional parks.

Location   The district of Metchosin and the municipalities of Colwood and Langford.

Length   27 kilometres.

Level   Easy to moderate.

Start   The Galloping Goose Trail's Park Avenue carpark.

Highlights   Rural countryside; Metchosin village church; views of the ocean and mountains; a possible side tour to Lester B. Pearson College.

How to get there Take Douglas Street/Trans-Canada Highway out of town. After 10 kilometres take the **R** Colwood exit onto the Old Island Highway (#14). (At Goldstream Avenue the road becomes Sooke Road.)

Continue for a further six or so kilometres until, at a sharp **L** bend and just past Happy Valley Road you turn **R** onto Glen Lake Road. Turn immediately **R** onto Park Avenue and the parking area for the Galloping Goose Trail.

THE RIDE

①		Exit the Park Avenue carpark turning **L** onto Glen Lake Road then **R** onto Sooke Road.
②	(0.09 km)	Turn **L** onto Luxton Road.
③	(2.9 km)	Turn **R** onto Happy Valley Road (Latoria Road is on the **L** at 2.8 km)
④	(6.2 km)	Turn **R** onto Lindholm Road.
⑤	(9.0 km)	Turn **L** onto Kangaroo Road.
⑥	(12.5 km)	Turn **R** onto Rocky Point Road.
⑦	(13.2 km)	Turn **L** onto Lombard Drive. (At .5 km along this road you'll come to an avenue of Lombardy poplar trees planted in 1903 by a local farmer, Henry C. Helgesen, as an approach to his farm.)
⑧	(14.0 km)	Turn **L** onto William Head Road. (If you turn **R** you'll end up either at the prison or at Lester B. Pearson College of the Pacific — the latter worth a visit.) Two hundred metres on the **R** is the entrance to Devonian Regional Park.
⑨	(15.9 km)	Pass through the village of Metchosin. Store and café are on the **L**. (The village church is a few metres past the corner store also on the **L**.)
⑩	(17.2 km)	Entrance to Witty's Lagoon Regional Park is on the **R**.
⑪	(20.9 km)	Turn **L** onto Latoria Road.
⑫	(22.6 km)	At the stop sign turn **R** onto the Veterans Memorial Parkway.
⑬	(25.1 km)	Turn **L** at traffic light onto Sooke Road.
⑭	(27.1 km)	Turn **R** onto Glen Lake Road as Sooke Road turns sharply **R** then **R** onto Park Avenue and the Galloping Goose parking area.

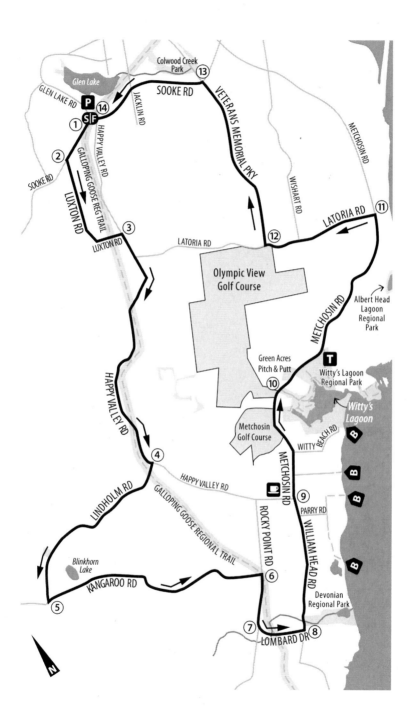

Glen Lake

Colwood Creek Park

SOOKE RD

GLEN LAKE RD

VETERANS MEMORIAL PKY

P

S/F

JACKLIN RD

SOOKE RD

HAPPY VALLEY RD

GALLOPING GOOSE REG TRAIL

LUXTON RD

LUXTON RD

WISHART RD

METCHOSIN RD

LATORIA RD

LATORIA RD

Olympic View Golf Course

Albert Head Lagoon Regional Park

METCHOSIN RD

HAPPY VALLEY RD

Green Acres Pitch & Putt

Witty's Lagoon Regional Park

T

Witty's Lagoon

GALLOPING GOOSE REGIONAL TRAIL

Metchosin Golf Course

WITTY BEACH RD

B

LINDHOLM RD

HAPPY VALLEY RD

METCHOSIN RD

B

B

Blinkhorn Lake

ROCKY POINT RD

PARRY RD

WILLIAM HEAD RD

KANGAROO RD

B

Devonian Regional Park

LOMBARD DR

N

METCHOSIN / EAST SOOKE

Don't be intimidated by the hilly nature of this route. It's a great ride and you'll get to see, close up, a number of the area's highlights. You'll start off rather sedately on the only road to Sooke. After the 17 Mile Pub though you venture into the hills. Your first plunge takes you down to sea level at Roche Cove. This small but lovely cove forms the western twin of two regional parks — Matheson Lake Park and Roche Cove Park. From the cove there are wonderful views of the Sooke Basin, and the surrounding hills hold some of the area's oldest cedars. As you ride along East Sooke Road you'll pass Becher Bay Road and the Aylard Farm entrance to the magnificent East Sooke Park. A visit here will not disappoint no matter what the season. The park is often described as a mystical place where the forest meets the sea and is regarded as the place where the West Coast truly begins. It's the largest of the regional parks and covers almost 1500 hectares. The Aylard Farm trailhead offers a picnic site and a small sandy beach. Not far past Becher Bay Road, Becher Bay will come into view on the right. Dotted with small islands, the bay focuses the eye on the open ocean and the mountains beyond.

You'll pass the entrance to two other parks — Matheson Lake Park and Witty's Lagoon Park. Both are worth a visit if time permits. If the hills become too much or time becomes limited there is always the Galloping Goose Trail to save you. You're never far from this trail and you cross it three times on this ride.

General description A longish loop route that takes you into the hills and along the shores of East Sooke and Metchosin.

Location Mostly in the districts of Sooke and Metchosin with a start in Langford.

St. Mary the Virgin in Metchosin.

Length   43 kilometres.

Level   Moderate to strenuous.

Start   The Galloping Goose Trail's Park Avenue parking area in Langford.

Highlights   The regional parks of Roche Cove, East Sooke, Matheson Lake and Witty's Lagoon; ocean and mountain views; Metchosin village and church.

How to get there   Take Douglas Street/Trans-Canada Highway out of town. After 10 kilometres take the **R** Colwood exit onto the Old Island Highway (#14). Follow the highway (which becomes Sooke Road) for about six kilometres until, at a sharp **L** bend, and just past Happy Valley Road **L**, you turn **R** onto Glen Lake Road. Turn immediately **R** onto Park Avenue. The parking area for the Galloping Goose Trail is just on your **R**.

THE RIDE

① From the carpark turn briefly **L** onto Glen Lake Road then **R** onto Sooke Road (Highway #14). Luxton fairground can be seen on your **L**.

② (9.0 km)   Kangaroo Road junction on the **L**.

③	(11.5 km)	17 Mile Pub is on your **R**.
④	(11.7 km)	Just after the pub turn **L** onto Gillespie Road.
⑤	(14.5 km)	Entrance to Roche Cove Regional Park is on the **L**. The Galloping Goose Trail crosses the road at this point.
⑥	(17.6 km)	Turn **L** onto East Sooke Road.
⑦	(19.6 km)	Becher Bay Road runs off to the **R**. The Aylard Farm entrance to East Sooke Regional Park is at the end of this road — a kilometre and a half away.
⑧	(24.5 km)	At the stop sign turn **L** onto Rocky Point Road.
⑨	(24.6 km)	Matheson Lake Road is on the **L**. This leads to the entrance to Matheson Lake Regional Park just over a kilometre away.
⑩	(25.0 km)	The Galloping Goose Trail crosses road.
⑪	(28.7 km)	Kangaroo Road junction on **L**. Also, the Galloping Goose Trail crosses here.
⑫	(29.8 km)	Turn **R** onto Happy Valley Road.
⑬	(30.4 km)	Metchosin village centre where there is a store, café and the old St. Mary the Virgin church. Turn **L** at the stop sign onto Metchosin Road.
⑭	(31.6 km)	Entrance to Witty's Lagoon Regional Park on the **R**.
⑮	(33.0 km)	Turn **R** onto Duke Road (West). (If you prefer not to take this short but pleasant detour, continue on Metchosin Road to ⑰. You'll save yourself 1.5 km.)
⑯	(33.6 km)	Turn **L** at the stop sign onto the continuation of Duke Road.
⑰	(35.4 km)	Turn **R** onto Metchosin Road.
⑱	(36.4 km)	Turn **L** onto Latoria Road.
⑲	(38.1 km)	Continue on Latoria Road past this signed junction with Veterans Memorial Parkway.
⑳	(40.2 km)	Turn **R** onto Happy Valley Road.
㉑	(42.4 km)	Turn **L** onto Sooke Road then immediately **R** onto Glen Lake Road and then **R** to the Park Avenue carpark of the Galloping Goose Trail.

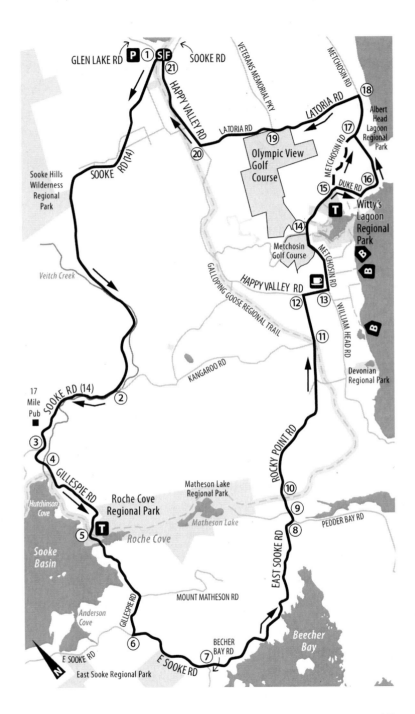

GLEN LAKE RD **P** ① **S** **F** ← SOOKE RD

SOOKE RD

VETERANS MEMORIAL PKY

METCHOSIN RD

LATORIA RD ②⑧

HAPPY VALLEY RD

LATORIA RD

LATORIA RD ⑲

Albert Head Lagoon Regional Park

⑳

⑰

SOOKE RD (14)

METCHOSIN RD

Olympic View Golf Course

⑯

Sooke Hills Wilderness Regional Park

⑮ DUKE RD

T

Witty's Lagoon Regional Park

⑭

B

Metchosin Golf Course

B

Veitch Creek

GALLOPING GOOSE REGIONAL TRAIL

HAPPY VALLEY RD

METCHOSIN RD

⑫ ⑬

WILLIAM HEAD RD

B

⑪

Devonian Regional Park

KANGAROO RD

17 Mile Pub ■

SOOKE RD (14) ②

ROCKY POINT RD

③

④ GILLESPIE RD

Roche Cove Regional Park

Matheson Lake Regional Park

⑩

Hutchinson Cove

Matheson Lake

⑨

PEDDER BAY RD

T ⑤

Roche Cove

⑧

Sooke Basin

EAST SOOKE RD

Anderson Cove

GILLESPIE RD

MOUNT MATHESON RD

Beecher Bay

N

E SOOKE RD ⑥

BECHER BAY RD

E SOOKE RD ⑦

East Sooke Regional Park

SOOKE / OTTER POINT / METCHOSIN

The road out to Sooke is deceptive. Not bad for a country road you might muse. A bit twisty perhaps, but no real hills. Fortunately or unfortunately, depending on your point of view, once you get past Sooke onto Otter Point Road and then, on the way back, you ride along Gillespie Road into East Sooke and Metchosin, the terrain changes — abruptly.

But before you get to the hills, you'll pass a couple of historically interesting sites. As you leave Colwood, about 14 kilometres into the ride you'll notice on your left the stone wall and gate house of Hatley Park — home of Royal Roads University and Hatley Castle. The castle and land once belonged to the late nineteenth and early twentieth century coal and railway baron, James Dunsmuir. Built in 1909, the castle was designed by the well known Victoria architect Samuel Maclure.

Dunsmuir hoped the castle would be the ancestral home of a dynasty of which his father Sir Robert Dunsmuir was the progenitor. It never happened and, in 1940, the federal government purchased the 228-hectare estate for $75,000. The park is open to the public and includes a variety of habitat including forest, lagoon, a creek as well as formal gardens.

The 17 Mile Pub on Sooke Road is one of three pubs and restaurants that sprang up along the road between Sooke and Victoria in the mid to late 1800s. The other two are the 4 Mile Pub and Restaurant in View Royal on the Old Island Highway and the Six Mile Pub, also on the Old Island Highway, in Colwood. (Actually, you pass it not long after leaving the Galloping Goose Trail.) These old "coachhouses" served to provide sustenance to early settlers who travelled between their farms in Sooke and Metchosin to and from Victoria.

Now, back to the hills. Otter Point Road traces a large arc from the centre of Sooke to the waters of the Strait of Juan de Fuca. It's only about 11 kilometres long but its hilly, twisty contours give a roller-coaster of a ride. Turning onto Gillespie Road at almost 70 kilometres into the ride you get the thrill of a steep descent to a bridge then the grunt of an uphill as the road travels toward Roche Cove. There are other ups and downs before the cove (which is also a regional park and worth a stop) and, as the route hits East Sooke Road and Rocky Point Road, the route gets no flatter. You have to wait until the 96 kilometre mark (where you're back on Sooke Road) before you can relax on a level road.

General description   This long excursion takes you into the beautiful rural communities that lie west of the city. Though not an easy ride, it explores some of the dramatic shorelines, with their attendant ups and downs, along the Strait of Juan de Fuca and the Sooke Basin. Along with the Malahat/Shawnigan Lake, the Galloping Goose Trail, the Cowichan Valley and the Jordan River rides, this is the furthest you'll get from downtown Victoria.

Location   Otter Point, Sooke, East Sooke, Metchosin and Victoria.

Length   111 kilometres.

Level   Strenuous.

Start   Galloping Goose Regional Trail's trailhead at the Johnson Street bridge in downtown Victoria.

Highlights   Hatley Park; 6 Mile and 17 Mile Pubs; regional parks; challenging and scenic country roads; views over ocean and mountains.

THE RIDE

①   From the Galloping Goose Regional Trail's trailhead at the Johnson Street bridge follow the trail to its intersection with the Trans-Canada Highway.

②   (4.0 km)   After crossing the Trans-Canada over the pedestrian/cyclist overpass (aka the Switch Bridge) turn **L** following the Galloping Goose Trail as it runs parallel to the highway.

③	(9.5 km)	At the trail's intersection with West Burnside Road and Watkiss Way, turn **L** onto the roadway of West Burnside riding under the highway to join the Old Island Highway as it runs through the sprawling suburbs of Colwood. After the junction with Goldstream Avenue the road becomes Sooke Road (Highway 14).
④	(14.5 km)	You pass the junction with Metchosin Road on your **L**. (You'll come back along that road many kilometres later.)
⑤	(30.0 km)	Just past the 17 Mile Pub **R** is the intersection with Gillespie Road **L** — another piece of pavement you'll become familiar with on your way back.
⑥	(38.3 km)	Sooke's town centre. Turn **R** here at the traffic lights onto Otter Point Road.
⑦	(49.6 km)	Moments before you hit this next checkpoint you'll know it's coming. At the top of a steep hill you see the ocean and the Olympic Mountains beyond. Turn **L** onto West Coast Road (Highway 14).
⑧	(61.4 km)	Continue through the traffic lights in Sooke. (Otter Point Road is off to your **L**.)
⑨	(69.6 km)	Turn **R** onto Gillespie Road. (The road is signed just before the turn.)
⑩	(75.3 km)	At the junction with East Sooke Road turn **L**.
⑪	(82.1 km)	A stop sign signals the end of East Sooke Road. Pedder Bay Road goes **R**, you turn **L** onto Rocky Point Road.
⑫	(87.5 km)	Turn **R** at the next junction onto Happy Valley Road.
⑬	(88.1 km)	After 600 metres turn **L** onto Metchosin Road. (The village centre is here.)
⑭	(96.5 km)	Turn **R** onto Sooke Road, direction Victoria.
⑮	(101.4 km)	As you see the overpass for the Trans-Canada Highway, move into the **L** lane to follow the signs for West Burnside Road. About 200 metres past the underpass and at the stop-signed intersection with Watkiss Way turn **R** onto the Galloping Goose Trail following it for about 10 kilometres back to the blue Johnson Street bridge.

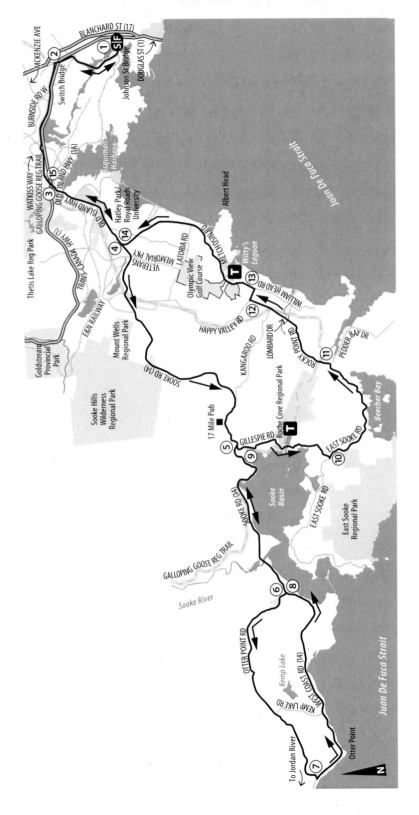

Roads and Trails

Over years of riding in and around Victoria I've poked my nose into all kinds of corners where I've suspected interesting off-road trails might exist. That curiosity has resulted in the short series of rides described below.

Most of us are familiar with the Galloping Goose and Lochside regional trails. The trails incorporated into these rides, though much shorter, will be a surprise to many. I've tried to create routes that include as much trail riding as possible in the hope that a combination of roads and trails will provide new, interesting and varied experiences. Thanks to the inclusive trail-use policies of surrounding municipalities and parks, many trails have now become multi-use. That has given us riders a much broader cycling environment.

On these rides you'll get to explore the upper reaches of Thetis Lake Park; connect the Mt. Work area, via the Hazlitt Creek Trail, with Gowlland Tod Provincial Park; you'll ride along Colquitz Creek as it passes Panama Hill Park and its neighbouring Panama Flats, and you'll even discover that the two halves of Bear Hill Road can become one — if you're on a bike.

The following routes are designed for hybrid, commuter, mountain and cyclecross bikes. The one exception is the ride that includes Thetis Lake where you'll need a mountain bike.

(Note: All the rides start and finish at the Johnson Street Bridge. At the time of writing, construction is underway on a new bridge. The Galloping Goose Trail trailhead therefore is rather hypothetical. I suggest you use the junction of Esquimalt Road and Harbour Road as your starting/finishing point.)

PENINSULA LOOPS

General description Three loop routes that wind through the Colquitz River Trail system and the rural landscape of the Saanich peninsula.

Location Saanich, Central and North Saanich and Victoria.

Length 65 km (Long Loop), 45 km (Medium Loop) and 28 km (Short Loop).

Level Moderate

Start Galloping Goose Trail trailhead on the west side of the Johnson Street Bridge.

Highlights Colquitz River Trail; Interurban Rail Trail; farm land of Saanich, Central and North Saanich; the Mills Road Trail and the Lochside Trail.

Long Loop (65 km)

THE RIDE

①		From the trailhead follow the Galloping Goose to the Switch Bridge over the Trans-Canada Highway.
②	(3.7 km)	Turn **L** keeping to the Galloping Goose. Cross Harriet Road and then Tillicum Road at the traffic light.
③	(4.9 km)	About 200 metres past Tillicum turn **R** down a signed side trail to Interurban Road. At the road turn **R**.
④	(6.1 km)	At the first light turn **R** onto Marigold Road then **L** after 50 metres onto the Colquitz River Park trail. (Pass Hyacinth and Panama Hill parks on your **R**.)
⑤	(77.7 km)	Cross Roy Road. (Unsigned.)
⑥	(8.1 km)	As the gravel ends turn **R** onto the unsigned Gerda Road and then, 20 metres on, **L** onto Grange Road.
⑦	(8.3 km)	Cross Carey Road onto the trail. Bear **R** immediately riding along the edge of Copley Park. (Colquitz Creek is on your **R**.)

⑧ (8.7 km) Cross Vanalman Road. After 100 metres enter a wooded area and cross a narrow, metal bridge and turn **L**.

⑨ (9.1 km) Turns **L** just before Eastridge Crescent and travel behind a row of houses for 300 metres to emerge onto Mann Avenue and turn **L**.

⑩ (9.8 km) At the light, cross Wilkinson Road. At the end of Mann enter and traverse Layritz Park on the Glendale Trail.

⑪ (10.6 km) Turn **R** at the large Centennial Trails map and descend to cross Markham Road onto the gravel trail. (It's a good idea to make walkers aware of your presence on the twisty section through the woods.)

⑫ (11.5 km) Turn **R** over a short bridge and sharp **L** as the trail ascends steeply to Quayle Road. (The Viaduct Flats viewing platform is on your **R**.)

⑬ (12.3 km) At Quayle turn **L** and then **R** onto the no-exit Elk Road. Follow Elk to its end where you turn **L** to cross Interurban Road at the cross walk.

For a shorter (28 km) ride see Short Loop page 130.

⑭ (13.4 km) Cross Interurban and take the signed Interurban Rail Trail going slightly to your **R**.

⑮ (17.0 km) The trail ends just past the Red Barn Market. Turn **L** onto Wallace Drive.

⑯ (20.7 km) Cross Benvenuto Avenue. (Butchart Gardens is to your **L**.)

⑰ (22.9 km) Now in Brentwood Bay, you turn **L** off Wallace onto West Saanich Road.

For a 45 km ride see Medium Loop page 128.

⑱ (33.4 km) Opposite the small Patricia Bay Park (you're now behind the airport runway) turn **R** onto the signed Mills Road trail.

⑲ (35.6 km) At the trail's end as it merges with McDonald Park Road continue on the road's bike lane to its intersection with the Pat Bay Highway.

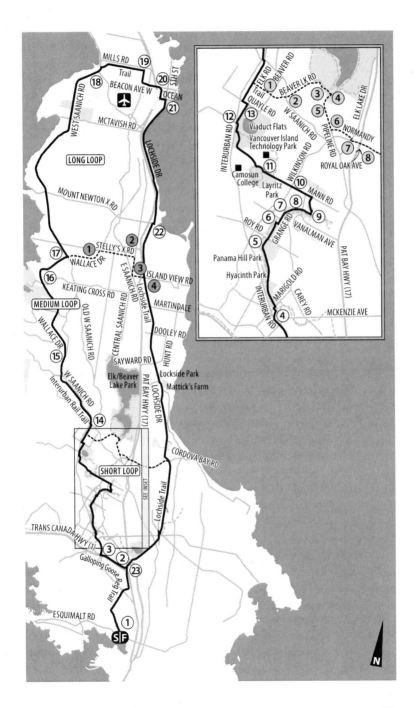

20	(36.6 km)	Cross the highway and turn immediately **R** over the slip road and take the paved Lochside Trail. You soon turn **L** riding to Ocean Avenue.
21	(37.8 km)	Turn **R** onto Lochside Drive. (Its bike lane is, in fact, the Lochside Trail.)
22	(44.2 km)	At the stop sign turn **R** onto Mt. Newton Cross Road and, 70 metres on, turn **L** onto the gravel section of the Lochside Trail. You now follow the trail through farmland and suburbs back to the junction at the Switch Bridge — some 17 kilometres.
23	(61.2 km)	Bear **L** to go over the bridge riding back to the route's start at the Johnson Street Bridge.

Medium Loop (45 km)

THE RIDE

Follow the main route to checkpoint (17). Instead of turning **L** onto West Saanich Road, cross the junction and continue on Wallace Drive.

1	(24.5 km)	Turn **R** at the four-way stop sign onto Stelly's Cross Road.
2	(26.0 km)	Stelly's ends at East Saanich Road where you turn **R**.
3	(26.8 km)	After passing the junction of Central Saanich Road on the **L**, turn **L** onto Island View Road riding down the steep hill to cross the Pat Bay Highway.
4	(27.2 km)	At Michell's barn turn **R** onto Lochside Drive (which is also the Lochside Trail). You now follow the trail back to the Switch Bridge junction (14 km away) where you turn **L** to take the Galloping Goose Trail back to the route's start at the Johnson Street Bridge.

Michell's Barn on the Lochside Trail.

Short Loop (28 km)

THE RIDE

Follow the main route to checkpoint ⑬. Instead of riding to the end of Elk Road turn **R** after about 400 metres onto Beaver Lake Road at 12.8 km. This short section of road soon becomes a trail into a wooded area.

①	(13.2 km)	Exit the trail and go straight on a continuation of Beaver Lake Road.
②	(13.5 km)	At the junction with West Saanich Road cross diagonally **R** to take another section of Beaver Lake Road.
③	(14.6 km)	Enter Elk/Beaver Lake Park
④	(14.9 km)	At the first bend and before the parking lot turn **R** onto a trail leading to Pipeline Road.
⑤	(15.1 km)	After crossing a wooden bridge, you emerge onto Pipeline Road.

How to beat the "Crawl."

<table>
<tr><td>⑥</td><td>(15.5 km)</td><td>Just before Pipeline ends, turn L onto Normandy Road.</td></tr>
<tr><td>⑦</td><td>(16.0 km)</td><td>Turn R onto Elk Lake Drive then immediately L at the traffic light onto Royal Oak Drive. Continue over the highway, past the shopping centre and into Broadmead.</td></tr>
<tr><td>⑧</td><td>(18.2 km)</td><td>At the first light turn R onto the Lochside Trail. You now follow the trail back to the Switch Bridge. Turn L to go over the bridge and ride to the route's start at the Johnson Street Bridge.</td></tr>
</table>

BEAR HILL /LAYRITZ PARK LOOP

General description A long-ish loop route that takes the rider along the Lochside Trail and then the Bear Hill, Elk/Beaver Lake and Layritz parks' trails.

Location Victoria, Saanich, Central Saanich and View Royal.

Length 46 kilometres.

Level Moderate.

Start Johnson Street Bridge/ Galloping Goose Trail trailhead.

Highlights Seabrook Road in Central Saanich; Bear Hill Road; the Glendale Trail through Viaduct Flats and Layritz Park.

THE RIDE

① From the Galloping Goose trailhead (on the west side of the Johnson Street Bridge), follow the signed trail for four kilometres to the Switch Bridge over the Trans-Canada Highway.

② (3.7 km) Over the bridge take the **R** fork. This is the beginning of the Lochside Trail. You'll stay on this trail as it crosses a number of major roads.

③ (13.2 km) Cross Cordova Bay Road at Mattick's Farm. Continue on the trail as you cross Hunt, Dooley and Martindale roads.

④ (18.6 km) Turn **L** off the trail onto Island View Road. (Michell's barn is on the corner.) Cross the Pat Bay Highway at the light and ascend the steep hill to turn **R** onto East Saanich Road.

⑤ (20.1 km) Turn **L** onto Stelly's Cross Road.

⑥ (20.7 km) At the top of the hill turn **L** onto Seabrook Road. At the end of Seabrook continue straight on a short gravel trail to connect with Oldfield Road.

⑦ (22.5 km) Keeping on Oldfield, cross Keating Cross Road. This stretch of Oldfield has farms, orchards and roadside produce stands.

⑧ (24.2 km) Watch for and turn **L** onto Bear Hill Road. It's marked "No Exit" but that's okay as you'll soon see.

⑨ (24.7 km) Turn **R** keeping on Bear Hill Road. (Signed for Bear Hill Regional Park.) At the end of the paved road (just past #5916) turn **R** onto a narrow gravel trail that leads to a continuation of Bear Hill Road.

⑩ (26.0 km) Cross Brookleigh Road at an awkward bend to continue on Bear Hill as it takes you into Elk Lake Park. You're soon on a very straight trail that travels along the park's west side.

⑪ (30.4 km) At the trail's end turn **R** onto Beaver Lake Road.

⑫ (31.0 km) Cross West Saanich Road diagonally **R** to take the continuation of Beaver Lake Road. (This is another awkward crossing.)

⑬ (31.4 km) At the T junction with Beaver Road continue straight to take a gravel trail into a wooded area. The trail exits onto a short section of pavement at the end of which you turn **L** onto Elk Road. After a brief gravel and paved section you intersect Quayle Road.

⑭ (32.3 km) Turn **L** onto Quayle and then, after about 70 metres, turn **R** onto the Glendale Trail. Keep to this trail past the Viaduct Flats and on up its wide gravel surface to Markham Road. (Camosun College is on the **R**, the Vancouver Island Technology Park on the **L**.)

⑮ (33.9 km) Cross Markham onto the paved trail that swings **L** to curve around a wooded knoll. You're now in Layritz Park.

⑯ (34.1 km) Continue straight at the Centennial Trails information board junction on a wide gravel trail. After 500 metres turn sharp **L** at another junction. (The Pacific Institute of Sports Excellence is straight ahead at this turn.) Continue to keep **L** until the gravel meets pavement where you turn **R** and **R** again to ride through the park's carpark. Exit the park on Layritz Avenue riding to its end. Turn **L** onto Glyn Road descending to Wilkinson Road.

⑰ (36.0 km) Turn **R** onto Wilkinson Road. Cross the Interurban/Hastings lighted intersection keeping to Wilkinson.

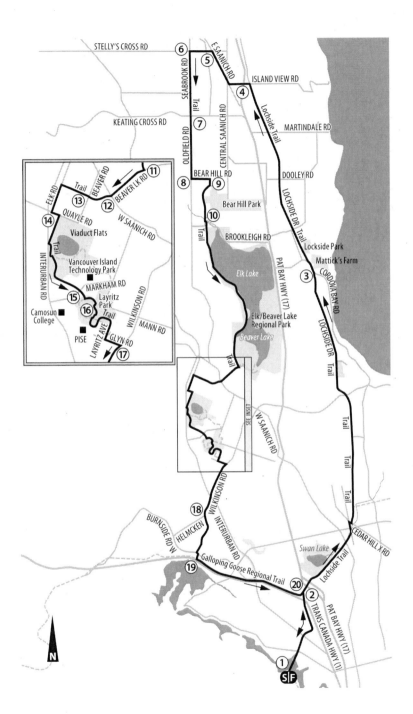

STELLY'S CROSS RD

SEABROOK RD

E SAANICH RD

ISLAND VIEW RD

⑥

⑤

④

Trail

KEATING CROSS RD

OLDFIELD RD

CENTRAL SAANICH RD

⑦

MARTINDALE RD

Lochside Trail

BEAR HILL RD

⑧ ⑨

DOOLEY RD

Bear Hill Park

⑩

BROOKLEIGH RD

Lockside Park

LOCHSIDE DR Trail

Mattick's Farm

Elk Lake

PAT BAY HWY (17)

③

CORDOVA BAY RD

Elk/Beaver Lake
Regional Park

Beaver Lake

LOCHSIDE DR

ELK RD

Trail

BEAVER RD

⑪

BEAVER LK RD

⑬

⑫

QUAYLE RD

W SAANICH RD

⑭

Viaduct Flats

Vancouver Island
Technology Park

INTERURBAN RD

Trail

MARKHAM RD

⑮

Layritz
Park

⑯

Trail

WILKINSON RD

MANN RD

Camosun
College

PISE

LAYRITZ AVE

GLYN RD

⑰

W SAANICH RD

Trail

SE 1st ST

WILKINSON RD

INTERURBAN RD

⑱

BURNSIDE RD W

HELMCKEN

Galloping Goose Regional Trail

CEDAR HILL X RD

Swan Lake

⑲

⑳

Lochside Trail

②

PAT BAY HWY (17)

①

TRANS CANADA HWY (1)

S F

N

(18)   (37.0 km)   At the next traffic light turn **L** onto a continuation of Wilkinson Road. (Straight ahead is Helmcken Road.)

(19)   (38.8 km)   Turn **L** onto Burnside Road West and then, after 20 metres, turn **R** down the no exit Belgrave Road. At the end of this short street turn **L** onto the Galloping Goose Trail.

(20)   (42.0 km)   After crossing McKenzie Avenue and Tillicum Road turn **R** at the trail junction to ride over the Switch Bridge and back to the ride's start.

Bridge on the Glendale Trail.

THETIS LAKE LOOP

General description A fairly challenging loop route that runs through Elk/Beaver Lake Park, along the Glendale Trail and Prospect Lake Road into the northern and western reaches of Thetis Lake Park. The quintessential Roads and Trails ride.

Location Saanich, View Royal and Langford.

Length 55 km and 48 km (Alternate Route).

Level Strenuous (mountain bike only).

Start Galloping Goose Trail trailhead west of the Johnson Street Bridge.

Highlights Viaduct Road West; some technical sections behind Francis/King Park and in the upper reaches of Thetis Lake Park; the alternative route on Thetis Lake Park's Trillium Trail.

THE RIDE

① From the trailhead, follow the Galloping Goose Trail to the Switch Bridge.

② (3.7 km) Once over the bridge take the **R** Lochside Trail. Keep to this trail for 10 km until a kilometre past Mattick's Farm.

③ (14.4 km) After a long avenue of trees turn **L** off the trail onto Hunt Road. Hunt quickly intersects Sayward Road. Turn **R** onto Sayward and climb up to the Pat Bay Highway. Cross the highway following the road as it bears **L**. At the Elk Lake Park sign turn **R** onto Brookleigh Road.

④ (17.3 km) At the top of a hilly bend turn **L** into Elk Lake Park on Bear Hill Road. This is the beginning of a long, wide section of trail, which you follow until its end.

⑤ (21.7 km) Turn **R** onto Beaver Lake Road.

⑥ (22.4 km) Cross West Saanich Road diagonally **R** onto a

continuation of Beaver Lake Road. At the first junction continue straight to take a marked, wooded trail. This narrow trail exits onto pavement at the end of which you turn **L** onto Elk Road.

⑦ (23.6 km) At the end of Elk turn **L** onto Quayle Road and then 70 metres farther turn **R** onto the marked Glendale Trail. Exit the trail at the entrance to the Viaduct Flats viewing platform onto Interurban Road — which you cross and take the hilly Viaduct Road West.

⑧ (26.0 km) Pass through the barriers at the end of Viaduct and take the narrow, rough trail on the **R** that leads to a continuation of Viaduct Road West. At the road's end turn **L** onto Prospect Lake Road.

⑨ (27.3 km) Watch for a power line clearing on your **R** at the end of which is a small turnout with a gate and barriers. Turn **R** through the barriers and take the wide track/trail under the power line. Keep to this main trail as it makes its way to Munn Road. (There's one technical section — a short gully — to negotiate.)

⑩ (28.9 km) Exit the trail onto Munn Road and turn **R**.

⑪ (30.1 km) Pass Rolla Place on your **R** and then, 200 metres farther, turn **L** onto a fire lane beside house #2359. After 30-odd metres bear **R** and take the gated rough fire road climbing **L**. (Despite its signage, this is a public right-of-way.)

⑫ (31.8 km) Coming off the (gated) fire road turn **R** onto Barker Road. Follow Barker to its junction with Westoby/Bate roads. Continue on Westoby and turn **R** as it terminates at a gated fire road. You're now at an entrance to Thetis Lake Park.

For the Alternate Route see next page.

⑬ (33.9 km) Ride around the gate on the trail marked Stewart Mountain. You soon turn sharp **L** onto the trail marked Thetis Lake.

⑭ (34.8 km) At the first trail junction turn **L** on the wide trail marked Thetis Lake.

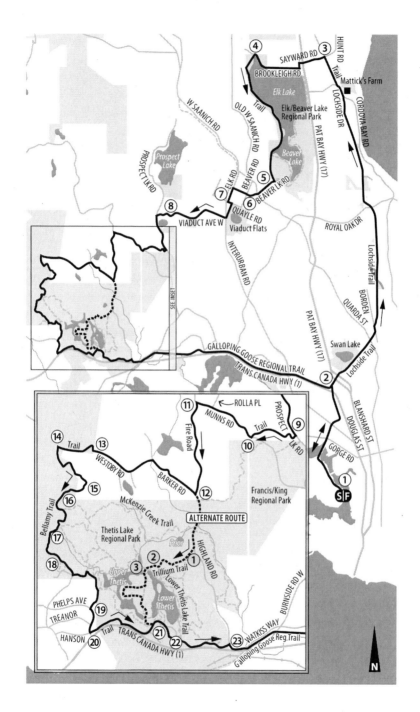

⑮	(35.7 km)	Turn **R** and **R** again at the next junction following the Thetis Lake trail.
⑯	(36.6 km)	Turn **R** onto the trail marked Thetis Lake. (To go straight is the McKenzie Creek Trail.)
⑰	(37.0 km)	At the next junction turn **R** onto the marked Bellamy Road trail.
⑱	(37.8 km)	Watch for the next trail going to your **L** marked Phelps Road/Thetis Lake. Follow this well-groomed single-track trail until you reach Phelps Road itself. (Actually, it's Phelps Avenue.)
⑲	(38.7 km)	Turn **L** onto Phelps Avenue. Keep to this paved road to its end.
⑳	(39.1 km)	Turn **L** onto a gravel trail into the trees. (You're now riding parallel to the Trans-Canada Highway.)
㉑	(40.4 km)	Exit the trail at the park's beach parking lot. Turn **R** to take the roadway to the park's main entrance.
㉒	(41.0 km)	As the entry road ends turn **R** onto Six Mile Road (the main road to the park) and, after 70 metres, take the ascending **L** trail.
㉓	(41.9 km)	The trail ends at Highland Road. Turn **R** and, after 200 metres, turn **R** again on a short, paved trail to join the Galloping Goose Trail and turn **L**. Continue on "The Goose" for 12 km to the route's end at the Johnson Street Bridge.

Alternate Route (48 km)

Follow the above route to checkpoint ㉒. Instead of turning **R** onto Barker Road, turn **L** onto Highland Road. Keep on Highland crossing McKenzie Creek bridge and passing a small parking area and trailhead on your **R**.

①	(32.7 km)	Turn **R** at the second parking area onto the marked Trillium Trail. (Cycling is permitted the length of this trail.)
②	(33.3 km)	At the first junction bear **R** on the trail marked Upper Thetis.
③	(33.5 km)	Continue straight at the next junction and then, after a few metres, turn **L** over a wooden bridge.

You keep to this trail until it descends and ends at the park's beach parking lot. Cross diagonally **R** to take the roadway to the park's main entrance.

You're now at checkpoint ⑳ on the main route. Follow that route description to complete the ride.

On the way to the trails.

HAZLITT CREEK LOOP

General description   A long, loop route that explores the heart of the Highland area. It takes in part of the Gowlland Tod Provincial Park and the municipality of Langford.

Location   Victoria, Saanich, Highlands, Langford.

Length   62 kilometres.

Level   Moderate to strenuous.

Start   Galloping Goose Regional Trail trailhead at the west end of the Johnson Street Bridge.

(Note: The original trailhead for this trail was the E&N train station at the east end of the bridge. Kilometre markers are measured from that point. That's why there's a discrepancy between my checkpoint kilometres and those on the official markers.)

Highlights   Ross-Durrance Road; Hazlitt Creek fire road; Gowlland Tod Park; the descent into Goldstream Park on Finlayson Arm Road; along Glen Lake on the Galloping Goose Trail.

THE RIDE

① From the Galloping Goose trailhead, follow the trail to its junction with the Lochside Trail just over the Switch Bridge.

② (3.7 km) Take the **R** fork and follow the Lochside Trail for a little over nine kilometres to its junction with Royal Oak Drive. (Lochside Elementery School is on the **R**.)

③ (9.4 km) Turn **R** onto Royal Oak Drive.

④ (11.9 km) Cross the Pat Bay Highway and pass through the traffic lights at Elk Lake Drive then turn **R** just before West Saanich Road onto Pipeline Road. Continue on Pipeline and then its trail into Elk/Beaver Lake Park.

⑤ (12.9 km) Exit the trail and turn **L** onto Beaver Lake Road. (The park entrance road.)

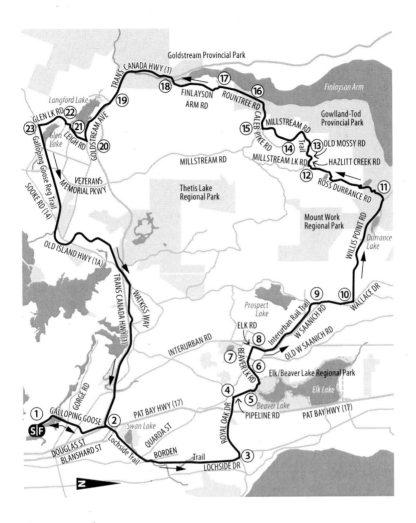

⑥ (14.0 km) As Beaver Lake Road meets West Saanich Road cross diagonally to your **R** to take the continuation of Beaver Lake Road.

⑦ (14.3 km) At the junction with Beaver Road take the trail ahead into a wooded area. This trail exits onto a roadway. After 50 metres or so, turn **R** onto Elk Road.

⑧ (15.4 km) Elk Road ends at the intersection of Interurban and West Saanich roads. You turn **L** and cross

Interurban at the pedestrian crossing and then, bearing **R**, take the gravelled Interurban Rail Trail.

⑨ (18.9 km) After passing the Red Barn Market on the **L** the trail ends at Wallace Drive onto which you turn **L**.

⑩ (19.4 km) Turn **L** onto Willis Point Road.

⑪ (23.5 km) Turn **L** onto Ross-Durrance Road.

⑫ (26.7 km) After a series of punchy hills turn **R** onto Hazlitt Creek Road.

⑬ (27.3 km) A little past Old Mossy Road (**R**) turn **L** through a gate onto a fire road which immediately crosses Hazlitt Creek itself. This steep rough-surfaced road climbs about a kilometre to Millstream Road.

⑭ (28.2 km) Turn **R** onto the butt-end of Millstream Road.

⑮ (31.4 km) Having passed Lone Tree Park on the **L** (30.1km) and after a fire hall on the **R**, turn **R** onto Caleb Pike Road. Follow this road into Gowlland Tod Provincial Park. Once in the park continue on a broad trail/fire road sweeping **L**.

⑯ (33.6 km) Pass through a gate and then 100 metres further turn **L** onto the poor surface of Rowntree Road.

⑰ (34.0 km) Turn **R** onto Finlayson Arm Road. This is a very steep and twisty descent to Goldstream Provincial Park and the Trans-Canada Highway.

⑱ (37.4 km) Turn **L** onto the Trans-Canada Highway.

⑲ (40.5 km) After the traffic lights at West Shore Way bear **R** onto Goldstream Avenue.

⑳ (42.1 km) Turn **R** onto Leigh Road. (The first main road after the highway.)

㉑ (43.1 km) A few metres before Leigh terminates at Langford Lake turn **L** onto a pathway that crosses railway tracks and the Langford Parkway and continues **R** through a small park up to Glen Lake Road.

㉒ (43.3 km) Turn **R** onto Glen Lake Road.

㉓ (44.5 km) Metres before Glen Lake Road meets Sooke Road turn **L** onto the well-signed Galloping Goose Trail. You now follow "The Goose" back to its trailhead at the Johnson Street Bridge — a distance of 18 kilometres.

Beyond
(Shawnigan Lake, Mill Bay, Cowichan Bay and the Cowichan Valley)

SHAWNIGAN LAKE /
CAMERON-TAGGERT ROAD

My first introduction to Shawnigan Lake was in the fall of 1980. I ran the (then named) Shawnigan Lake Road Race — an almost 23 kilometres race that circumnavigated the lake. I have long forgotten the pain of running that race but the memory of the beautiful autumnal colours of the trees along the course, the vistas over the lake and the picturesque lakeshore homes and cottages has remained firmly in my mind all these years. I have since ridden and run around the lake many times but my favourite season to do so is the fall. However, no matter when you ride the lake it will inevitably be a splendid experience.

Shawnigan Lake has always been a favourite spot for Victorians to visit. For years the (now defunct) Shawnigan Lake Resort, at the lake's north end, was a well-known place to stay and vacation. The private Shawnigan Lake School has occupied its ivy-covered main buildings set amongst formal gardens since 1916. You'll get a glimpse of the school about a kilometre from the end of the ride.

At the Lake's village you'll find a museum dedicated to the

pioneering spirit of the area, and an array of stores and cafés. Cameron-Taggert Road, besides being a lovely bucolic backroad, is the only way to the province's first estate cidery. The Merridale Cidery, at the end of Merridale Road, is reputed to produce "the best English-style cider in Canada." Like their cousins, the local vineyards, they offer tastings in a rustic farmhouse and give tours of the orchard, apple mills, presses and fermentation casks.

West of the lake is an abandoned CN railway line (now part of the Trans-Canada Trail). For the railway to span the Koksilah River, a huge trestle was constructed which had the reputation as being one of the world's highest and longest. Known as the Kinsol Trestle, it has long been condemned for travel but is still a favourite tourist attraction.

General description   The longest portion of this ride is a loop around Shawnigan Lake. What is added is a smaller loop that takes you toward Cobble Hill then back along a quiet country road and on through the village of Shawnigan Lake.

Location   Shawnigan Lake, 45 kilometres north-west of Victoria.

Length   22 or 32 kilometres.

Level   Moderate.

Start   Mason's Beach parking area .5 km north of Shawnigan Lake Village.

Highlights   Beautiful lake; rural road with light traffic; provincial park with beach and picnic area; possible visit to a cidery; possible side trip to the Kinsol Trestle.

How to get there   Take Douglas Street/Trans-Canada Highway out of town. Continue on the highway up and over the Malahat to Mill Bay. At the second set of traffic lights turn **L** onto Shawnigan Lake-Mill Bay Road. After nine kilometres and at the junction with East Shawnigan Road and Renfrew Road in Shawnigan Lake Village turn **R** onto Renfrew Road. After half a kilometre, turn **R** into the gravel parking area to Mason's Beach just before the intersection of Shawnigan Lake Road.

Cyclists waiting for the Brentwood Bay/Mill Bay ferry.

THE RIDE

① From the parking area turn **R** onto Renfrew Road then **R** again onto Shawnigan Lake Road.

② (3.2 km) Turn **R** onto Cameron-Taggert Road. After 50 metres continue **R** on the same road.

③ (5.0 km) To the **L** is Merridale Road, the location of the Merridale Estate Cider company.

④ (6.9 km) Turn **R** onto Shawnigan Lake–Mill Bay Road.

⑤ (10.0 km) At Shawnigan Lake Village turn **L** at the stop sign onto East Shawnigan Lake Road.

⑥ (12.4 km) Less than a kilometre after passing under a railway bridge turn **R** onto Stowood Road. You'll avoid a nasty hill this way. Also, you'll pass a restaurant and marina — if you're interested in a bite to eat — and lakeside cottages.

⑦ (13.3 km) Turn **R** to rejoin the main road.

⑧ (18.1 km) At the end of the lake turn **R** onto West Shawnigan Lake Road.

⑨ (24.9 km) On the **R** is the entrance to the West Shawnigan Lake Provincial Park.

⑩ (27.5 km) Turn **R** onto Renfrew Road. (To view the Kinsol Trestle, billed as one of the world's longest and highest trestle bridges, turn **L** here and ride the kilometre and half to its trailhead and then the short distance to the trestle.)

⑪ (31.9 km) Ride past Mason's Beach on your **R** and the grocery store and junction with Shawnigan Lake Road on the **L** turning **L** into the Mason's Beach parking area.

(For a shorter ride — by 10 kilometres and avoiding the Cameron-Taggert loop — turn **L** out of the start's parking area riding the .5 km back to the village and circumnavigate the lake clockwise [see **⑤** above].)

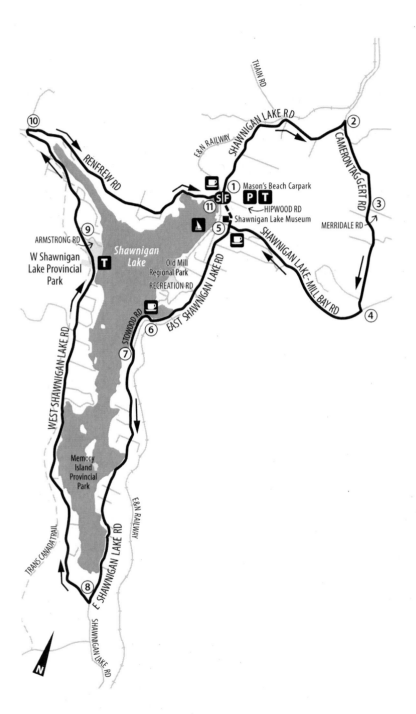

SHAWNIGAN LAKE VIA THE MALAHAT DRIVE

A little shy of a hundred kilometres this ride is often regarded by local cyclists and triathletes as the proving ground on which to base their fitness and race preparedness.

I've started the ride on Blanshard Street (which morphs into the Pat Bay Highway on the outskirts of town) because of its wide boulevard and generous bike lane. The almost three kilometre out section along McKenzie Avenue is safe for the experienced rider as is the Trans-Canada Highway which has a very usable shoulder. The stretches on the Galloping Goose Trail are, because of their paved surface, ideal and safe.

The two defining sections of this long ride are the Malahat Drive and the ride out of Shawnigan Lake up the six kilometre Shawnigan Lake Road hill to the Malahat. The Malahat Drive portion of the Trans-Canada Highway that you ride is a little over eleven kilometres. Both the above hills are quite relentless but both have portions that are flattish — meaning you can catch your breath.

Although you don't ride the whole length of the Malahat and its summit of 356 metres is only a few kilometres past the Shawnigan Lake South turn-off, its history is interesting. Named after the local First Nation people — the Malahat — and, notwithstanding that a trail of some kind has existed over this protrusive piece of land for millennia, the first thoroughfare of any width was a cattle trail that was cut in 1861. As commerce became more important between the Cowichan Valley area and the fledgling community of Victoria, the trail evolved, by 1884, into a wagon road. The road was finally paved in 1911. Over the century since the road has gone through many improvements and upgrades. *It is a beautiful stretch of road especially if one looks east. There you see over the Saanich Inlet to the Saanich Peninsula with the radar towers atop Mount Newton boldly dominating its north end, and beyond are the Gulf Islands. Another mount — Mt. Finlayson — looms large on the skyline as you descend into Goldstream Park on the journey back.*

General description One of the longest and most challenging rides in the book. But it offers so much. In addition to a good workout, you'll get great views over the Saanich Inlet, ride through a portion of Goldstream Park, circumnavigate the picturesque Shawnigan Lake and have bragging rights over your less energetic friends.

Location Trans-Canada Highway as it heads out of Victoria, Malahat Drive, Shawnigan Lake.

Length 97 kilometres.

Level Strenuous.

Start Downtown Victoria on Blanshard Street.

Highlights The Malahat Drive; views east over the Saanich Peninsula and beyond; the 22 kilometre ride around Shawnigan Lake; Shawnigan Lake village.

THE RIDE

①   From downtown ride Blanshard Street then out to the Pat Bay Highway to McKenzie Avenue. A good dedicated bike lane begins after the intersection with Caledonia Avenue — a little over a kilometre from Blanshard Street's start.

②   (5.7 km)   Take the **R** McKenzie off ramp signed "Nanaimo/ Sooke" turning **L** onto McKenzie Avenue.

③   (8.5 km)   As McKenzie intersects the Trans-Canada Highway turn **R** onto the Galloping Goose Regional Trail. (An alternate route is to begin at ride #32's start and follow the Galloping Goose Trail to this point.)

④   (13.4 km)   At the trail's intersection with West Burnside Road and Watkiss Way, cross over onto Watkiss Way itself riding almost parallel to the highway for a little over .5 kilometre taking a short, paved trail on the **L** up to the wide shoulder of the highway. Continue on the highway passing Goldstream Provincial Park which marks the beginning of the Malahat Drive.

⑤ (32.7 km)   Roughly two kilometres after a gas station and restaurant on your **R**, turn **L** onto Shawnigan Lake Road about 70 metres past the Shawnigan Lake South sign.

⑥ (38.9 km)   After descending the long steep hill and turning **R** (with Sooke Lake Road going to the **L**) you turn **L** onto West Shawnigan Lake Road. You'll now circumnavigate the lake in a clockwise direction.

⑦ (48.2 km)   The road terminates at a stop sign where you turn **R** onto Renfrew Road.

⑧ (53.1 km)   Ride through the centre of Shawnigan Lake village onto East Shawnigan Lake Road.

⑨ (61.2 km)   Leaving the lake you now retrace your ride bearing **L** up the six-kilometre hill of Shawnigan Lake Road to the Trans-Canada Highway (aka the Malahat Drive).

⑩ (67.1 km)   Turn **R** onto the highway.

⑪ (86.1 km)   Turn **R** onto the well signed exit 11 View Royal/ Colwood off-ramp. At the bottom of the ramp turn **R** onto Six Mile Road and after 200 metres turn **L** onto Atkins Road. As Atkins ends, turn **R** and continue on to the Galloping Goose Trail riding its 10 kilometre length back to Victoria to finish at the Johnson Street bridge.

MIA CROUCH

Malahat Summit view.

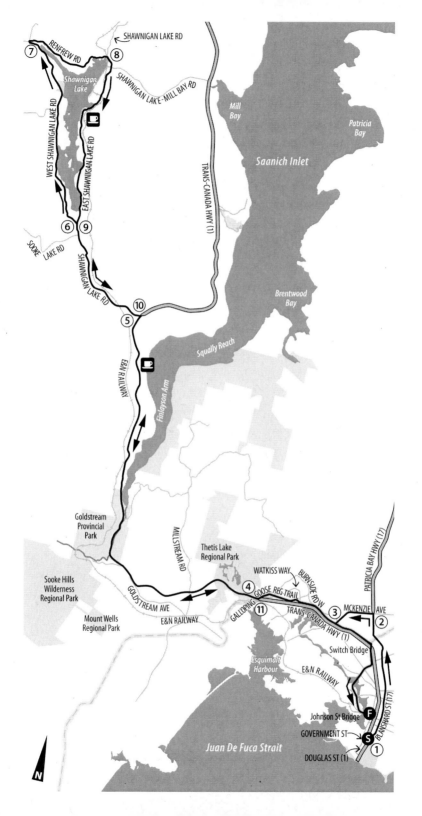

MILL BAY / COWICHAN BAY /
SHAWNIGAN LAKE

Embarking as it does at the end of a short ferry trip, this ride has the feeling of a mini adventure. You'll ride through three small settlements and get a good taste of the pastoral nature of the rather extensive Cowichan Valley. You start by riding through the small village of Mill Bay situated at the north end of the famous Malahat Drive. As you might expect, the village derives its name from a lumber mill that was built on the bay during the late 1800s. It's now largely a retirement settlement and the well-known private school, Brentwood College, sits overlooking the bay.

As you ride north you enter the Telegraph Road/Cherry Point area. A major attraction is the Cherry Point Vineyards. Once a mink farm, Wayne and Helena Ulrich bought the property in the late 1980s and, by stint of hard

labour, transformed the gravelly and, in parts, hard clay land into a productive vineyard. Since the spring of 2004, the vineyard has been owned and operated by the First Nation's Khowutzun Development Corporation — a wholly-owned subsidiary of the Cowichan Tribes. They grow premium grapes that produce well-respected Pinot Noir, Pinot Gris, Gewertraminer and other varieties.

Further north you ride down the steep hill into Cowichan Bay village. The present day village site was originally a Hudson's Bay Company fort back in the 1850s and was second only to Victoria as a European settlement on Vancouver Island. In 1862 the British HMS Hecate arrived in the bay full of settlers who began to farm, trap and eventually fish and log. In the early 1900s the village was a bustling tourist destination

with steamboats calling at the dock bringing sight-seers and vacationers. The present-day Masthead Restaurant was once the Columbia Hotel which was built around 1868.

On your route back you'll ride by Cobble Hill village and into Shawnigan Lake village. There you'll find a small museum, a selection of stores and cafés and, if you have time, a beach area for a picnic.

General description A mini-adventure into the countryside north of the Malahat and south of Duncan. Includes a ferry ride with the possibilities of wine and cheese tasting.

Location Mill Bay, Cowichan Bay, Cobble Hill and Shawnigan Lake.

Length 47 kilometres.

Level Moderate (one major hill).

Start Mill Bay Ferry terminal five kilometres south of Mill Bay Centre.

Highlights Brentwood Bay/ Mill Bay Ferry ride; Cherry Point Vineyards; Hillary's cheese farm; Cowichan Bay; Shawnigan Lake.

How to get there Follow Blanshard Street/Pat Bay Highway (#17) out of town. Take the Keating Cross Road exit **L** at about 15 kilometres. Continue on Keating for another 3 kilometres turning **R** onto West Saanich Road. Drive through Brentwood Bay's traffic light and turn **L** after 500 metres onto Verdier Avenue down to the Brentwood Bay Ferry terminal. There is ample parking 100 metres on the **R** before the ferry dock. A store and café are located close to the terminal. Remember to check the ferry schedule for your return journey.

Alternate route to Mill Bay Ferry terminal: From Victoria drive up and over the Malahat (Trans-Canada Highway) turning **R** onto Mill Bay Road at about 40 kilometres from Victoria's downtown. (This is also the turn-off for Bamberton Provincial Park.) The Mill Bay ferry is 1.5 kilometres along this road. There is good parking just past the access road to the ferry on the water side. Start your computer from where you park. You should hit the Mill Bay Centre/Deloume Road at about 5 kilometres.

THE RIDE

① From the Mill Bay ferry terminal ride up the approach road for 300 metres and turn **R** onto Mill Bay Road.

② (5.5 km) Turn **L** onto Deloume Road (the Mill Bay Centre is on the **L** just before this junction) and, after 100 metres turn **R** at the traffic light onto the Trans-Canada Highway.

③ (7.2 km) After a short stretch of highway turn **R** at the traffic light onto Kilmalu Road.

④ (7.8 km) Turn **L** onto Telegraph Road.

⑤ (14.0 km) Turn **R** onto Cherry Point Road.

⑥ (15.0 km) On the **L** is the entrance to Cherry Point Vineyards. After the entrance bear **L** to follow Cherry Point Road.

⑦ (18.4 km) Halfway down a steep hill on the **L** is a farm selling Hillary's Fine Cheeses which are highly regarded by the locals.

⑧ (18.7 km) Turn sharply **L** at the bottom of the hill. You're still on Cherry Point Road.

⑨ (20.1 km) Turn **R** onto Cowichan Bay Road.

⑩ (21.5 km) At the bottom of a 15% grade hill you enter the village of Cowichan Bay. There are restaurants, stores, cafés and a marina here. To continue your ride return to the base of the hill and turn **R** onto Wilmot Road. This is a steep hill that twists and turns for almost a kilometre and eventually intersects Koksilah Road. (The Trans-Canada is on your **R**.)

⑪ (23.6 km) Turn **L** onto Koksilah Road (not signed).

⑫ (25.5 km) Turn **R** onto Telegraph Road.

⑬ (26.3 km) Turn **R** onto Cowichan Bay Road.

⑭ (28.5 km) Cross the Trans-Canada Highway onto Cobble Hill Road.

⑮ (31.1 km) To the **L** is Cobble Hill village. On the **R** is the Cobble Hill railway shelter for the rail-line between Victoria and Courtenay. Shortly after the village Cobble Hill Road veers to the **L**. You continue straight on what is now Shawnigan Lake Road.

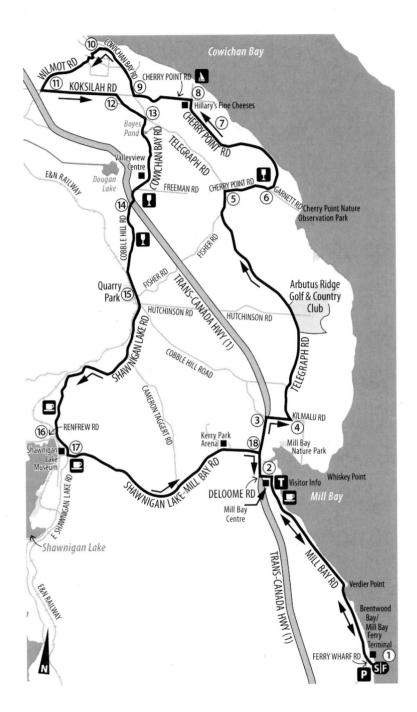

Cowichan Bay

WILMOT RD

COWICHAN BAY RD

⑩

⑪ KOKSILAH RD

⑨ CHERRY POINT RD

⑧

⑫

⑬

Boyes Pond

CHERRY POINT RD

Hillary's Fine Cheeses

⑦

TELEGRAPH RD

E&N RAILWAY

Valleyview Centre

Dougan Lake

FREEMAN RD

COWICHAN BAY RD

CHERRY POINT RD

GARNETT RD

Cherry Point Nature Observation Park

⑭

⑤ ⑥

COBBLE HILL RD

FISHER RD

FISHER RD

Arbutus Ridge Golf & Country Club

TRANS-CANADA HWY (1)

Quarry Park ⑮

FISHER RD

HUTCHINSON RD

HUTCHINSON RD

SHAWNIGAN LAKE RD

COBBLE HILL ROAD

TELEGRAPH RD

CAMERON TAGGERT RD

③ KILMALU RD

④

Kerry Park Arena

Mill Bay Nature Park

RENFREW RD

⑯

⑰

⑱

② Whiskey Point

Shawnigan Lake Museum

SHAWNIGAN LAKE–MILL BAY RD

DELOOME RD

Visitor Info

Mill Bay

E. SHAWNIGAN LAKE RD

Mill Bay Centre

Shawnigan Lake

E&N RAILWAY

TRANS-CANADA HWY (1)

MILL BAY RD

Verdier Point

N

Brentwood Bay/ Mill Bay Ferry Terminal

FERRY WHARF RD ①

P S F

⑯ (35.9 km) Turn **L** as the road intersects Renfrew Road. Mason's Beach is across the road.

⑰ (36.4 km) After a gradual uphill turn **L** at the stop sign in Shawnigan Lake village onto Shawnigan Lake-Mill Bay Road.

⑱ (41.9 km) Turn **R** onto the Trans-Canada Highway and then after .5 km turn **L** onto Deloume Road. (Mill Bay Centre is on your **R**.) After 100 metres turn **R** onto Mill Bay Road riding the 5 kilometres or so back to the ferry terminal.

Trail map at the Kinsol Trestle.

COWICHAN VALLEY WINERY TOUR

Imagine. Sunlight glinting on vine leaves. Row upon row of maturing, luscious grapes on vines rising like marshalled troops on the rolling hillside. The day's breeze tickling your arms and legs as you pedal along winding lanes. For all the world, you could be in Italy's Tuscan hills or France's Bordeaux region or even California's Napa Valley. But you're not. You're cycling through one of the continent's finest and fastest growing wine areas — the Cowichan Valley.

This tour will take you to seven of the region's vineyards — each with its own special attractions. Most will offer food as well as wine tastings.

The ride is about 30 kilmetres long and can be accomplished nicely in half a day. For those who want a more leisurely pace, there are a number of B & Bs en route. (Tourism Cowichan's website is in the index.)

The Cowichan Valley is also known for its large dairy farms and smaller hobby farms — both make for beautiful scenery and give a sense you're in the heart of the country.

I've started the ride from the Valleyview Centre shopping mall just off the Trans-Canada Highway. It's a convenient place to park your car and a stone's throw away from the first of the day's vineyards.

General description This ride will introduce you to one of the treasures of southern Vancouver Island — the Cowichan Valley. Besides visiting seven of the region's finest vineyards you'll ride by beautiful farmland along winding country roads. There are ample rest stops and grand views of the surrounding countryside.

Location About 50 kilometres north of Victoria on both sides of the Trans-Canada Highway.

Length 30 kilometres.

Level   Easy to moderate.

Start   The Valleyview Centre shopping mall 50 kilometres north of Victoria at the intersection of the Trans-Canada Highway and Cowichan Bay Road **R** and Cobble Hill Road **L**.

Highlights   Vineyards; light traffic; rolling countryside; accessible refreshments and accommodation.

How to get there   From Victoria leave town on the Trans-Canada Highway. A few kilometres past Mill Bay turn **R** onto Cowichan Bay Road at a traffic-lighted intersection. The entrance to the Valleyview Centre is 200 metres on your **L**. (For more information about the Cowichan Valley see the website in the Index.)

THE RIDE

① From the Valleyview Centre carpark turn **R** onto Cowichan Bay Road. After 300 metres cross the Trans-Canada Highway onto Cobble Hill Road.

② (1.0 km) Entrance to the *Glenterra Vineyards* is on your **L** and 400 metres further, on your **R**, is the *Silverside Farm and Winery*.

③ (2.7 km) Pass Cobble Hill Village on your L and then turn **L** 200 metres later onto a continuation of Cobble Hill Road.

④ (6.2 km) With the École Mill Bay on your **L**, the road turns sharply **R**. The length of Cobble Hill Road is bordered with hobby farms, large and small.

⑤ (7.3 km) Cross the Trans-Canada Highway onto Kilmalu Road. Four hundred metres later turn **L** onto Telegraph Road.

⑥ (9.3km) After a couple of kilometres along this lumpy but delightful country road you see the *Enrico Winery* on your **L**.

⑦ (10.5 km) Just off the road on your **L**, at the junction of Hutchinson Road, is the *Damali Lavender Farm, Winery and B&B*.

⑧ (14.2 km) Turn **R** onto Cherry Point Road.

⑨ (15.3 km) The *Cherry Point Vinyard* are on your **L**.

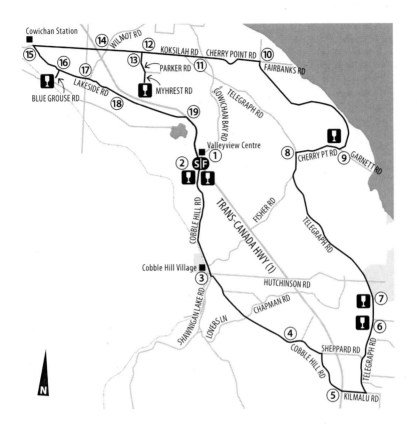

⑩	(18.7 km)	Pass Hilary's Fine Cheese's farm. The company's store is in Cowichan Bay Village. Three hundred metres further the road turns sharply **L**.)
⑪	(20.3km)	Cross Cowichan Bay Road onto Koksilah Road.
⑫	(22.1 km)	Turn **L** onto Parker Road and then **R** onto the narrow Myhrest Road at the end of which is the *Rocky Creek Winery*.
⑬	(23.3 km)	Retrace back to Koksilah Road and turn **L**.
⑭	(24.1 km)	Cross the Trans-Canada Highway (again). Ignore the first sign for the *Blue Grouse Estate Winery*.
⑮	(25.7 km)	Turn **L** onto Lakeside Road. (Cowichan Station is a little further on Koksilah.)

⑯ (26.62 km) Turn **R** onto the short, gravel Blue Grouse Road to the *Blue Grouse Estate Winery*.

⑰ (27.0 km) Back on Lakeside you pass the Sunrise Waldorf School on your **R**.

⑱ (28.0 km) Lakeside bears **R** to parallel the Trans-Canada for a kilometre.

⑲ (29.1 km) Turn **R** to join the highway riding the two kilometres back to the ride's start at Valleyview Centre.

Trails

Galloping Goose and Lochside Regional Trails

We can thank the entrepreneurial vigor and pioneering vision of both the national and local railway builders for the two long regional trails of greater Victoria that are their legacy.

Believe it or not, shortly after the turn of the twentieth century, there were five working railways that ran out of Victoria to service Sooke, the Saanich Peninsula, Nanaimo, Port Alberni and Courtenay.

The longest and the one still in existence, is the Esquimalt and Nanaimo (E&N) line that runs as a passenger service between Victoria and Courtenay — a town 234 kilometres to the north. It started operations in 1883 and eventually reached Courtenay in 1914.

The line for the "Galloping Goose" gas-powered railcar. was developed by the Canadian Northern Pacific Railway (which became the Canadian National Railway in 1918). It had its first run in 1922 carrying mail and a maximum of 30 passengers from Victoria to Sooke. Although the line continued to Cowichan Lake, the passenger service to Sooke ended in1931. However, the freight service to Cowichan continued until the 1950s. The Goose's 55 kilometre portion of the line was acquired by the Capital Regional District in 1987 and opened to the public as a trail a year later. Much work has been done on the trail over the years with its first 10 kilometres good quality pavement.

The Lochside Trail was once one of three railway lines that ran up the Saanich Peninsula. To compete with the British Columbia Railway Company (BCRC) which ran up the west side of the peninsula (started in 1912) and the Victoria and Sidney Railway (V&S) (started in 1894), which ran up the middle, the Canadian Northern Pacific Railway (CNPR) chose, in 1915, to build a line on the peninsula's eastern side. Although all three lines met their demise during the economically depressed 1930s, stretches of each exist today as trails for our use — the CNPR line being the Lochside Trail.

I've deliberately departed from the format of the rest of the rides in this book since both trails are linear and you can't get lost. But here are a few suggestions for rides along particularly interesting sections of these flat trails (for those not wanting to ride their whole lengths). Suggested rides are indicated by letters.

Trail etiquette: *keep right except to pass; sound your bell or shout "bike" to let others know you're coming; control your speed; be aware of pedestrians, horse riders and other cyclists; respect the environment.*

On the "Goose" at Railyard.

GALLOPING GOOSE REGIONAL TRAIL
(110 kilometres)

For those wanting a shorter ride than the whole trail, here are three suggestions:

(A) Starting at the 18 kilometre mark next to the Luxton Fairgrounds ride to Roche Cove Regional Park. This section offers views of the ocean, tree-lined and grassy-verged sections and the chance to visit Matheson Lake for a dip and/or a picnic. (34 kilometres out and back)

(B) For a shorter version of the above, start just before the Kilometre 30 mark on Rocky Point Road riding above the shores of Matheson Lake to Roche Cove. (10 kilometres out and back)

(C) Just before the 44 kilometre point at the parking area off Sooke River Road (the trail crosses the road here) travel north riding over the two sweeping trestle bridges over Charters and Todd Creeks. This section to Leechtown follows the Sooke River very closely at times and you'll get a chance to pause at the restored Barnes Station on the way about seven kilometres in. As you approach the trail's end at Leechtown (a long-abandoned gold-mining settlement at the confluence of the Sooke and Leech Rivers) there are a number of choice picnic spots by the river. (22 kilometres out and back)

(For information on B&Bs close to the Goose go to the website in the index.)

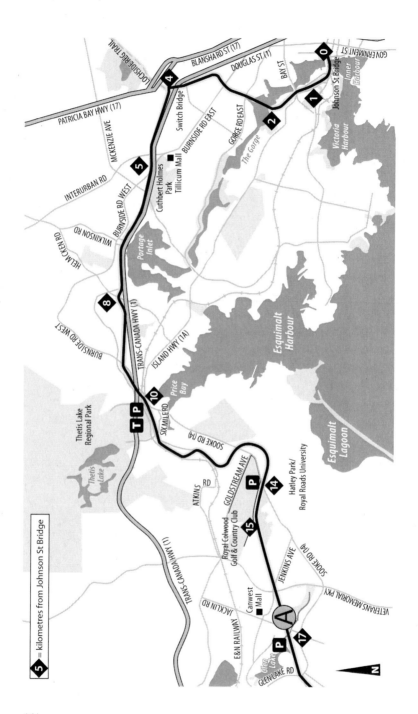

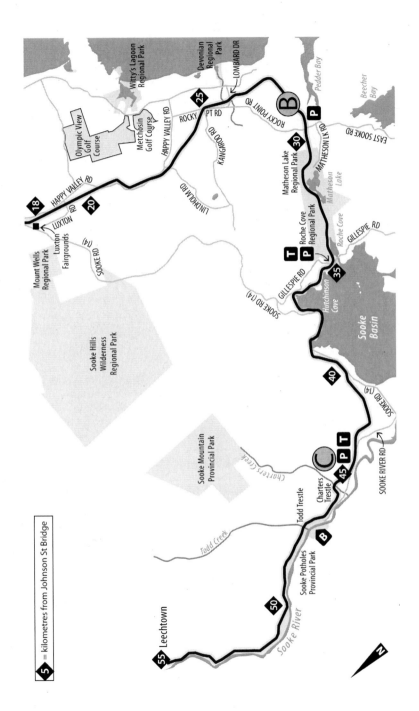

LOCHSIDE REGIONAL TRAIL
(66 kilometres)

For those wanting a shorter ride than the whole trail, here are two suggestions:

(A) From the trail's parking area on Lochside Drive just north of McKenzie Avenue ride over the 288 metre-long Blenkinsop Trestle and then along the side of Cordova Ridge on Lochside Drive to finish at Mattick's Farm for tea or coffee. (15 kilometres out and back)

(B) Begin your ride at Lochside Park. From here ride along the avenue of trees and then into the open farmland paralleling the Pat Bay Highway. Continue along Lochside Drive passing Cy Hampson Park at around the 25 kilometre mark and then ride to the oceanside Tulista Park, which marks the entrance to the town of Sidney. If you want to explore the town, ride the extra kilometre to the town's main street — Beacon Avenue. (26 kilometres out and back)

Traffic on the Selkirk Trestle.

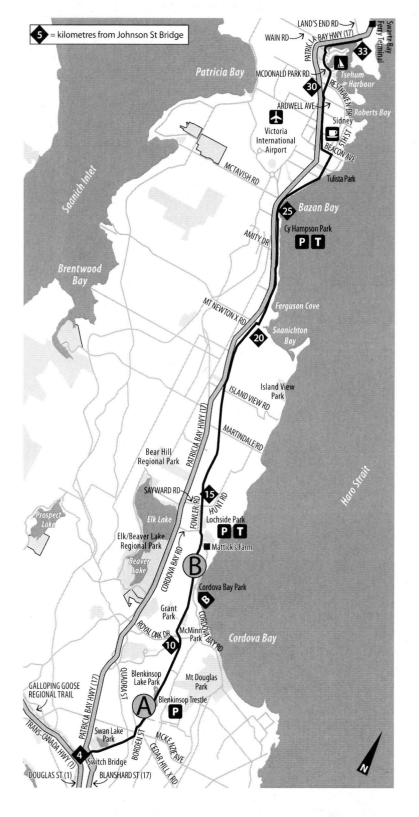

On the Kinsol Trestle.

TRANS-CANADA /
COWICHAN VALLEY TRAIL

The highlight of this ride is undoubtedly at its end — the Kinsol Trestle. Reopened in 2011 after being condemned for 30 years as being unsafe, this impressive structure is one of the longest wooden trestles in the world.

After almost 14 kilometres of riding, the Kinsol Trestle comes into view — a gently curving complexity of wooden beams that spans the Kinsol Valley and the Koksilah River below.

The trestle was built in 1914 as part of the Canadian National Railway that went from Victoria to Nanaimo via Lake Cowichan. The line was an ill-conceived project; it was unable to compete with the Esquimalt & Nanaimo Railway built around the same time and was abandoned after only a few years in operation.

The name "Kinsol" is a contraction of King Solomon, the rather pretentious name given to a copper mine that opened in the early 1900s on the banks of the Koksilah River.

As with riding the Galloping Goose Trail, riding this section of the Trans-Canada Trail (also known as the Cowichan Valley Trail) evokes the sensation of going back in time. The time when behemothic steam engines pulled loaded railcars along kilometres of tree-lined tracks; plumes of gray smoke belching out the engines' smoke-stacks and the wheels clickety-clacking along the rails. Today, the line is a well-groomed gravel trail that allows people, not goods, to travel along a quiet, largely wooded corridor not far from the shores of Shawnigan Lake.

You can now ride across the trestle and follow the Cowichan Valley Trail to its end on the shores of Lake Cowichan — if you want.

General description An out-and-back ride along a heritage trail on the west side of Shawnigan Lake.

Location Shawnigan Lake, 40 kilometres north of Victoria.

Length 28 kilometres.

Level Easy.

Start Sooke Lake Road access point to the Trans-Canada Trail. (Also known as the Cowichan Valley Trail.)

Highlights The Kinsol Trestle at the end of the ride; the much shorter trestle over McGee Creek; a possible return route through Shawnigan Lake village.

How to get there Take Douglas Street/Trans-Canada Highway out of town. At about 31 kilometres and just before the crest of the Malahat turn **L** onto the well-signed (South) Shawnigan Lake Road. After another six kilometres turn sharp **L** onto the gravel Sooke Lake Road at the very bottom of a steep hill. A kilometre and half farther turn **R** into the parking area of the beginning of the Trans-Canada Trail.

THE RIDE

①		From the Sooke Lake Road access parking area ride north along a well-defined, wide trail.
②	(5.0 km)	Access road with a picnic table.
③	(6.2 km)	Gate.
④	(6.7 km)	Cross the McGee Creek Trestle.
⑤	(9.3 km)	Cross Oland Road (gated).
⑥	(9.8 km)	Cross Sallachie Road (gated).
⑦	(11.8 km)	Cross Renfrew Road (gated).
⑧	(12.4 km)	Cross Shelby Road (gated).
⑨	(12.7 km)	Approach to Kinsol Trestle (gated).
⑩	(13.7 km)	Kinsol Trestle. As of 2011, you can now cross the trestle and extend your ride for as long as you want for an out-and-back — even as far as Lake Cowichan (a further 40 kilometres!). The return route can be either retracing your entire ride out or returning to Renfrew Road (⑦) turning **L** and riding back via Shawnigan Lake Village, East Shawnigan Lake Road and the short section of Sooke Lake Road back to your car. (This will add only another 3 or 4 kilometres to your ride.)

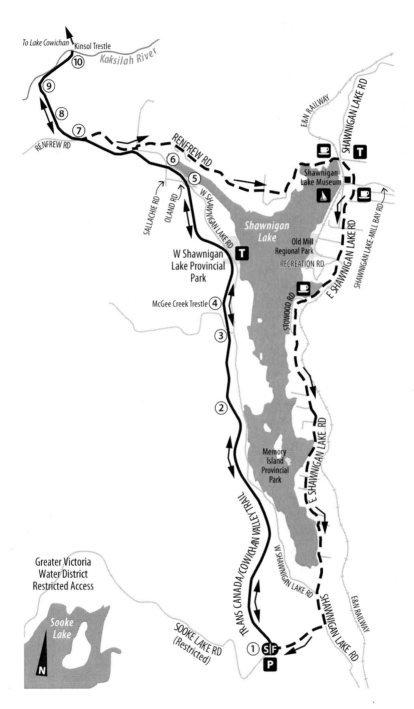

To Lake Cowichan Kinsol Trestle
(10)
Koksilah River

(9)

(8)

(7)
RENFREW RD

RENFREW RD

SALLACHIE RD

OLAND RD

(6)

(5)

W SHAWNIGAN LAKE RD

E&N RAILWAY

SHAWNIGAN LAKE RD

Shawnigan
Lake Museum

SHAWNIGAN LAKE RD

SHAWNIGAN LAKE-MILL BAY RD

Shawnigan
Lake

W Shawnigan
Lake Provincial
Park

Old Mill
Regional Park

RECREATION RD

E SHAWNIGAN LAKE RD

McGee Creek Trestle (4)

STONWOOD RD

(3)

(2)

Memory
Island
Provincial
Park

E SHAWNIGAN LAKE RD

TRANS CANADA/COWICHAN VALLEY TRAIL

W SHAWNIGAN LAKE RD

E&N RAILWAY

SHAWNIGAN LAKE RD

Greater Victoria
Water District
Restricted Access

Sooke
Lake

N

SOOKE LAKE RD
(Restricted)

(1) S F
P

171

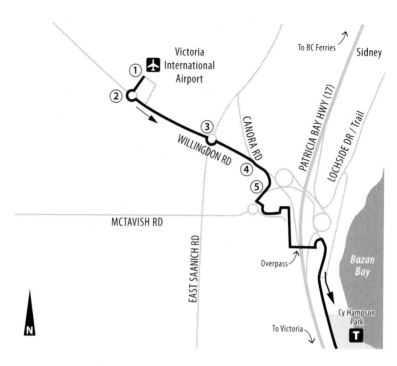

Victoria
International
Airport

To BC Ferries
Sidney

WILLINGDON RD

CANORA RD

PATRICIA BAY HWY (17)

LOCHSIDE DR / Trail

MCTAVISH RD

EAST SAANICH RD

Overpass

Bazan
Bay

To Victoria

Cy Hampson
Park

N

Routes to Victoria
from Victoria International Airport and Swartz Bay Ferry Terminal

VICTORIA INTERNATIONAL AIRPORT

For those arriving at either the Victoria International Airport or the Swartz Bay Ferry Terminal *and want to cycle into Victoria, the following are four suggested routes.*

THE RIDE

① Exit the parking area riding **R** past the airport's Arrivals doors.

② (.04 km) At the first roundabout turn **L** (signed "To Victoria.") and keep to the bike lane.

③ (1.4 km) Continue past second roundabout.

④ (1.6 km) Willingdon becomes Canora Road.

⑤ (2.1 km) At the third roundabout turn **R** and follow the paved path signed for the Lochside Trail. In following the path you'll cross the highway and an off-ramp on an overpass. (This looks complicated but it isn't.) As you meet Lochside Drive/Trail turn **R** riding the pleasant and relatively quiet 25 kilometres into downtown Victoria.

SWARTZ BAY FERRY TERMINAL

THE RIDE

① After walking your bike off the ferry ride along the terminal's main exit road and either: Ⓐ continue as the road becomes the Pat Bay Highway (#17) riding the 30-odd kilometres on the highway's wide shoulder to Victoria or Ⓑ ride for about 300 metres and turn sharp **R** 50 metres past an overpass onto a well marked bike path. (A good map of the suggested route into Victoria is at this point.)

② Continue on this path for 50 metres and turn **R** to ride over the overpass.

③ Ride through the traffic lights at the end of the overpass.

④ A further 50 metres turn **R** onto Curteis Road following the signs of the **Lochside Trail** for 32 kilometres to Victoria.

Note. The Lochside Trail joins the Galloping Goose Trail at the Switch Bridge (which crosses the Trans-Canada Highway) with four kilometres remaining of your journey. The blue Johnson Street bridge marks the end of the trail. You're on the edge of downtown Victoria now. If you turn **R** once over the bridge onto Wharf Street you'll find the Victoria Tourist Bureau on your **R** as Wharf intersects Government Street (and opposite the Empress Hotel).

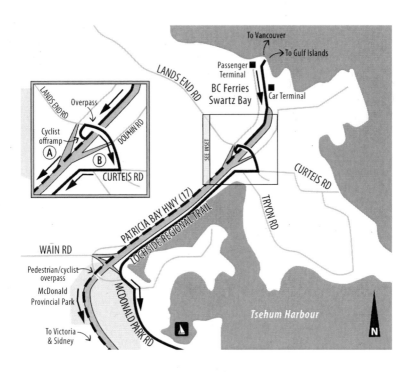

The Lochside Trail near the Swartz Bay Ferry Terminal

Index

Rides by distance

Rides between 31 to 50 kilometres

Resources

Websites

www.tourismvictoria.com
www.gvcc.bc.ca
www.crd.bc.ca/parks
www.tourismcowichan.com
www.capitalbikeandwalk.org
www.southvanislebnb.com

The Author

John Crouch is a well-known local author. His three guidebooks, *Walk Victoria*, *Hike Victoria* and the first edition of *Bike Victoria*, have become, and remain, best sellers.

Besides cycling, John is a prolific walker and hiker. Over the past few years he's hiked the John Muir Trail in California (including Mt. Whitney — the tallest peak in the lower 48), routes in Snowdonia and the Lake District in the UK, and in the national parks of Wyoming, Utah and Nevada.

In the summer of 2011, John cycled, solo, from Whitehorse in the Yukon, 2,500 kilometres to his home in Victoria.

Despite all his activities, John enjoys spending time with his wife, his children and his grandchildren.

Other guidebooks by John Crouch:
Walk Victoria and *Hike Victoria*

To order copies of these books go to:
www.bikewalkvictoria.com